Building Dynamic Business Communities

This book is based on the author's lengthy experience in creating communities and helping organizations and individuals thereby provide for evangelism and sustained growth. The result is dynamic marketing and sales at low, or no, cost of acquisition. Thus, communities are powerful sources for business owners, executives, and entrepreneurs. The research and literature supporting communities and the power of referral, peer-level influence, and normative buying pressures are enormous. This is not an internet-based or "pyramid marketing" initiative, which is based on a zero-sum game and is unethical or illegal. These communities are both "live" and remote; and become perpetual-motion sales machines. Most organizations have the raw material for successful communities, but they don't realize it, nor do they know how to go about creating them.

This work is the remedy. The author believes that many people are still "lonely" and isolated post-pandemic with remote work or hybrid work. Communities can embrace these people to build camaraderie and higher performance. The key benefits include *gaining value for merely bringing people together who normally would never have met or rarely meet*; providing viral marketing among members of entrepreneurial communities, which is effective 24/7; easily creating global communities to expand business; and dramatically building brands. Essentially, this book will enable the reader to use over a dozen pragmatic, sequential steps to organize resources, publicize, gain members, provide instant value, and assemble critical mass for the community to continually add members and perpetuate itself in "The chain reaction of attraction"®.

Building Dynamic Business Communities

How to Create an Evergreen Client Ecosystem

Alan Weiss, PhD

A PRODUCTIVITY PRESS BOOK

First published 2025
by Routledge
605 Third Avenue, New York, NY 10158

and by Routledge
4 Park Square, Milton Park, Abingdon, Oxon, OX14 4RN

Routledge is an imprint of the Taylor & Francis Group, an informa business

ISBN: 978-1-032-83019-3 (hbk)
ISBN: 978-1-032-87978-9 (pbk)
ISBN: 978-1-003-50732-1 (ebk)

DOI: 10.4324/9781003507321

Typeset in Garamond
by Apex CoVantage, LLC

This is dedicated to Gaby, Ace, Everleigh, and Max, our grandchildren.

As my father-in-law, a wonderful man, used to say,

"What else is as important as seeing your grandchildren grow up?"

So here's something for my family's community: The children who know me, the grandchildren who will know me but not as well, and their descendants who won't know me at all except through my work and legacy.

This one's for you, with love.

Contents

PART TWO Creating A Community

Figures

Foreword

In Winnetka, Illinois, I walked into the mansion of my girlfriend's house, at the time. It was amazing, the biggest house I'd ever been in! After meeting her parents I asked her father what he did for a living. Instead of explaining his job (pharmaceutical salesforce effectiveness consulting)—that's a mouthful—he gave me a copy of Alan's *Million Dollar Consulting.* He said, "This will change everything for you."

It did.

Fast-forward to today: I help run AppSumo.com with nearly 100 million in yearly revenue. Alan was a key inspiration and educator in the success of my company.

And if you go back to the beginning of AppSumo, it started with just one customer who spent $12 to start. And that one customer turned into a community of solopreneurs who love affordable tools to help grow their own businesses. Most people are incorrectly focused on tactics, strategies, mindsets, and whatever to try to "shortcut their way" to riches. But the real success is in building your community one by one. Helping other people. Simple.

But how to do it?

Luckily, Alan is STILL doing it with his own community.

And in this book he shows how to come up with your ideas for community, how to launch, and how to thrive with your community. I love that he shows how to do this with real stories, action items, and clear messaging.

Community is the most important element in business growth. I look forward to you building out your own community with Alan's help.

—Noah Kagan

—Author, *Million Dollar Weekend*

Acknowledgments

No book on community could be credibly written without the full support of the members of a dynamic and long-term community from around the world. My thanks to you all.

I especially appreciate the second generation of some of you who have also joined the community. But I'm drawing the line at the third!

About the Author

Alan Weiss is one of those rare people who can say he is a consultant, speaker, and author *and mean it.*

His consulting firm, Summit Consulting Group, Inc., has attracted clients such as Merck, Hewlett-Packard, GE, Mercedes-Benz, State Street Corporation, Times Mirror Group, The Federal Reserve, The New York Times Corporation, Toyota, and over 200 other leading organizations.

He has served on the boards of directors of the Trinity Repertory Company, a Tony-Award-winning New England regional theater, chaired the Newport International Film Festival, and been president of the board of directors of Festival Ballet Providence (now Ballet RI).

His speaking typically includes 20 keynotes a year at major conferences, and he has been a visiting faculty member at Case Western Reserve University, Boston College, Tufts, St. John's, the University of Illinois, the Institute of Management Studies, Highpoint University, and the University of Georgia Graduate School of Business. He has held an appointment as an adjunct professor in the Graduate School of Business at the University of Rhode Island, where he taught courses on advanced management and consulting skills to MBA and Ph.D. candidates. He once held the record for selling out the highest-priced workshop (on entrepreneurialism) in the then-21-year history of New York City's Learning Annex.

His Ph.D. is in psychology. He has served on the Board of Governors of Harvard University's Center for Mental Health and the Media.

He is an inductee into the Professional Speaking Hall of Fame® and the concurrent recipient of the National Speakers Association Council of Peers Award of Excellence, representing the top 1 percent of professional speakers in the world. He is a Fellow of the Institute of Management Consultants, one of only two people in history to hold both designations.

His prolific publishing includes over 500 articles and 60 books, including his best-seller, *Million Dollar Consulting* (from McGraw-Hill), now in its 32nd year and sixth edition. His latest prior to this one was *Sentient Strategy* (Routledge, 2023). His books have been on the curricula at Villanova, Temple University, and the Wharton School of Business and have been translated into 15 languages.

His career has taken him to 60 countries and 49 states. (He is afraid to go to North Dakota.) *Success Magazine* cited him in an editorial devoted to his work as "a worldwide expert in executive education." The *New York Post* called him "one of the most highly regarded independent consultants in America." He is the winner of the prestigious Axiem Award for Excellence in Audio Presentation.

He is the recipient of the Lifetime Achievement Award of the American Press Institute, *the first-ever for a non-journalist, and one of only seven awarded in the 65-year history of the* association. He has coached former candidates for Miss Rhode Island/Miss America in interviewing skills. He once appeared on the popular American TV game show *Jeopardy*, where he lost badly in the first round to a dancing waiter from Iowa.

Alan is married to the lovely Maria for 56 years, and they have two children and four grandchildren. They reside in East Greenwich, Rhode Island, with their dogs, Coco, and Royce, a white German Shepherd.

Introduction

With the publication of my fourth book, *Million Dollar Consulting* (McGraw-Hill) in 1992 (it's currently in its sixth edition), I began an unintended shift from the corporate (wholesale) marketplace to the consumer (retail) marketplace. And I discovered I had inadvertently created and was sustaining a community.

Few of us today do not live in one kind or another of "community." A community is generally described as a "group of people with common beliefs and/or common geography." Hence, there are communities that are global (and, for all we know, cosmic) that never interact in person, abetted by increasingly remote and virtual communications. There are also communities that are solely about live, daily interactions, such as "Koreatowns" or Chinatowns" within many US cities. There are examples of members of these communities not speaking English at all, but rather shopping, communicating, raising families, banking, working, and so forth strictly in their own languages and with their own customs.

The name could be said of Hasidic Jews or the Amish, of little-known groups in the Amazon rainforest, or of indigenous peoples living within the Arctic Circle. In countries as disparate as Italy and China one can go over a hill or through a forest and find a dialect of the common language that is indecipherable to a visitor, as well as vastly different customs and food preparations.

The first community in recorded history is considered to be the Sumerian, in the fourth century BC. The oldest civilizations usually recognized are those of Mesopotamia, Egypt, China, and the Indus Valley. This makes sense considering that most scientists agree that modern human ancestors arose in Africa about 200,000 years ago. (The oldest *continuous* culture is thought to be that of aboriginal Australians, still occupying its original geography 65,000 years later.)

The Christian population grew by 40 percent a decade, from about 1,000 Christians in the year 40 to 7,530 in 100 to a little over six million in 300 and 33 million in 350, growing, in the hundred years between 250 and 350, from about 2 percent of the population to slightly over 31 percent of all affiliated religious groups today. There are three reasons generally considered to be the main causes for this kind of completely unprecedented growth: the belief that Jesus was the Messiah (the Jews thought He was still to appear), the uniformity of the Christian ceremony (pagan ceremonies differed widely), *and the practice of community help for members, such as aid for the sick, the injured, and the destitute, which was without prior practice.*

Don't confuse "community" with "tribe," although many people use the terms interchangeably (and incorrectly). A community is heterogeneous, inclusionary, tends to be diverse, doesn't require intimacy or close sharing, and is usually based on broad, common values, such as freedom, ethics, and individual rights.

Tribes tend to be exclusionary and homogeneous, demand tight conformance to rules and rituals, and may require high degrees of sharing and intimacy. It has a hierarchy which may be hereditary or based on power. There is one religious belief, an enclosed society, and one culture (no Chinatowns allowed). Consequently, they are often indigenous and usually have a shared proximity and personal interaction.

These terms, of course, have evolved and been contorted over modern times. Seth Godin, an author and marketing strategist, speaks commonly of "tribes" and has written a book by the same name[1] (along with dozens of others). He's a bright guy and speaks of people in tribes as connected to a leader, each other, and an idea. I urge you to also consider his viewpoint.

However, I believe we easily form tribes, change them (a rock group goes out of existence, pickleball will run its course the same way platform tennis did), and belong to several concurrently. The tribe may concern a single leader (Jim Jones) or a single idea (Starbucks as elitist coffee) but may or may not have any further influence on members outside of that issue or person.

But communities are more complex, can be sustained and grown with the introduction of new values and innovation, *and are underappreciated and underutilized as supporters of lives and businesses.* There are exceptions, such as communities of those sharing a common disease or hardship, which are appreciated and superbly utilized by those in need. But we've tended to neglect our customers and clients and sometimes find, by accident, that we have a community of potentially rabid supporters.

And when we learn this, we don't know what to do about it.

I Do. Read on.

—Alan Weiss
November 1, 2024

NOTE

1 *Tribes*, Penguin Group, 2008.

Part One

Community Origins and Strengths

1

The Nature of the Modern Socio-Business Community

In the increasingly virtual, separate, and isolated post-pandemic world there is a growing need for socialization and informal business exchange. People are "Zoomed-out" and have become "Zoom potatoes"! This vacuum can be filled with huge benefit to everyone, most especially the "community organizer."

I was once flabbergasted that Barack Obama, a highly popular, two-term president, had as his major resume item "community organizer"! "How plebian," I thought. It turns out, of course, that these skills and talents were exactly what was needed for a relatively unknown without a distinguished Senate record, to easily win the presidency.

KINDRED AND UNKINDRED SPIRITS

As we become more aware of (but not necessarily accustomed to) a far more detached and remote world, we lose a sense of "connection." Ironically, the very tools and technologies which enable us to remain in contact virtually also serve to isolate us personally. This isn't entirely caused by the pandemic, which exacerbated previously existing angst.

These are some traditional sources of community:

- The family dinner table
- Service clubs and organizations (Lions, Elks, Rotary, and so forth)
- Trade and professional associations
- Private clubs

DOI: 10.4324/9781003507321-2

- Coherent groups (alumni associations, book clubs, hobby enthusiasts, adult learning centers)
- Informal and amateur athletics (golf, tennis, pickleball)
- Neighborhoods and towns (parades, recreational facilities, civic meetings, school boards, dog parks)
- Professions and jobs (offices, teams, after-work socializing)
- Health and fitness (gyms, pools, stables)
- Poor health and lack of fitness (rehab centers, hospitals, self-help groups, weight and diet control)
- Volunteerism (community watch and security, food banks, building restoration)

You probably have some to add, and you can see that this is a significant list, with people able, historically, to forge bonds, connections, friendships, and relationships.

But let's look at these today, as dispassionately as possible:

The Family Dinner Table: This has virtually disappeared as a daily occurrence. Two-income and single-parent families have changed the way the household works. Even with traditional, "intact" families, extracurricular activities, holding down two jobs or working overtime, an astonishing variety of recreational options on the internet, and both a daily commute and occasional (or more often) travel for work have pretty much eviscerated the immediate and/or extended family from sharing food at one time at one table.

Service Clubs: Rotary is losing about 10,000 members a year. All of the major service clubs are in significant decline. People don't have the time, and younger generations have not seen the appeal. In his 2000 book, Bowling Alone: The Collapse and Revival of American Community,[1] Robert Putnam documented that attending club meetings, such as those held by Rotary and Kiwanis groups, had already declined by 58 percent in the period 1975–2000. This trend continued and even accelerated in the twenty-first century. Putnam notes it's part of an overall trend by Americans who also have 43 percent fewer family dinners, as well. Thirty-five percent fewer of us have friends who drop in to see us at our homes. That was from 24 years ago, which is why I've pointed out that the pandemic merely exacerbated what was already in motion.

Trade and Professional Associations: The era of "12 monthly magazines and a convention" is over. People are not willing to pay dues and commit time (even Zoom time) for boring publications and "talking heads." There are about 44,000trade and professional associations in the US, with assuming 500 members on average, 22 million members, generating $36billion annually in revenue.[2] (Numbers aren't exact because any individual can belong to more than one association. Even at an average of 100 members, we're talking about almost 5 million members.) In 1922, for example, 11%of these organizations declined, 25%experienced zero growth, and the remaining 32% grew by 5% or less. Younger generations aren't joining these groups, and people weary of (or afraid to) travel are dropping out. Virtual association meetings are largely ineffective. And for some organizations built around historic circumstances, this is even worse. The American Legion, the famous veterans organization, has lost over 700,000 members over the past ten years, and the VFW (Veterans of Foreign Wars) lost 200,000 people between 2017 and 2021 alone.[3] (These are huge drops even removing deceased members from the numbers.) Ironically, the AARP (American Association of Retired People), which ought to be expanding in terms of power given an aging population, is far too often concerned not with representing seniors but in selling things to them. They have failed completely at creating a community.

Private Clubs: Private golf clubs, for example, are suffering from the changing demographics of the country, competition from public courses which charge only a fraction of private courses, and changing lifestyles and technology. After 121 years, the University Club of Albany's remaining 62 members (from a high of overl,000) had to sell the building. Younger people are looking for more diversity in their lives, and the considerable fees and dues are perceived to be best applied elsewhere.

Coherent Groups: These groups, too, are suffering from old age. Toy train collectors, philatelists, numismatists, and so forth are not appealing to younger generations. (Even the Rolls Royce Club and Bentley Club recently combined!) Alumni associations, which remain large and growing, too often see members treated as ATM machines for their former universities. The magazines have dwindled to online newsletters, which, in turn, have been reduced to a few updates on university awards and grants. The Yale and Princeton Clubs in New York City are in decline.

Informal and Amateur Athletics: This category has a positive report. Public golf courses have expanded the numbers of weekend golfers, and sports such as pickleball, which can be played quite well in middle age and beyond, are blossoming. Communities form around clubs, regular games, and the players. This is also true in the health and fitness arena, mentioned below. However, much of this is transitory. Platform tennis was once all the rage and has almost disappeared. Will pickleball follow?

Neighborhoods and Towns: Even in large cities, there are neighborhoods (and suburbs) that create community with local culture, wellness, dining, entertainment, transportation, and so forth. (If you ever want to witness tribal culture, just take a commuter train on a daily basis for a week.) These people do come together for neighborhood improvement, school issues, social justice issues, and crime prevention. This also applies to "over-50 communities," "no children communities," and so forth.

Professions and Jobs: Community is formed in some offices, which include office celebrations (marriage, birth, promotion) and gatherings after work, be they in a gym or a bar. However, remote and hybrid work has seriously undermined these activities and so has the increasingly horrible traffic around most cities. People want to get home fast if they are in the office all day. Boston restaurants suffer (and are closing) because workers don't favor returning to the city for dinner with the lack of surface transportation and tangled traffic.

Health and Fitness: This industry suffered terribly during the pandemic but has bounced back, only to face new obstacles, such as Peloton, home gyms, and higher costs. Because it's such a competitive market, they can't raise their prices to meet the higher rates of rent, insurance, and new equipment. In my observation, communities aren't formed here; they're really just temporary meeting places where people are too busy to really talk.

Poor Health and Lack of Fitness: I think it's clear that groups such as Alcoholics Anonymous form long-term communities based on common values and mutual help—the idea of "sponsors," for example. However, the current movements against "body shaming" and insisting that all sizes and shapes are fine and are even healthy have undermined the weight-loss and exercise industries. Moreover, the advent of drugs created for other reasons (e.g., Ozempic, created to deal with

Type 2 diabetes) which have proved to help reduce weight have made this pursuit very personal and private.

Volunteerism: People volunteering for charities, arts groups, civic cleanup, and so forth do tend to form communities, but mainly with those who are not actively employed and otherwise engaged. It's difficult enough to get volunteers to board meetings, or soup kitchens, or municipal meetings without expecting them to get together for social reasons, as well.

Remember the Shriners, the men with the fez hats who rode around in tiny cars and raised money for Shriners Hospitals and free medical care? There are about 300,000 today, down from over a million about 25 years ago.

Dan Gilbert, a retired professor of psychology at Harvard University, found in his research[4] that people who admitted to being active church attendees scored higher on happiness scales than those who did not. But people who specified they believed in God were no happier on the scales than those who did not believe. He attributed that to the church being a community of common values, people who frequently saw each other, and the church being a social center beyond being solely a religious one. I asked him over a scotch if it might be that happier people simply tended to attend church more than those who were unhappy.

"Well, that could be," he said.

It is harder and harder to find and sustain kindred spirits today unless we make a concerted effort to do so.

THE POWER OF PEER-LEVEL REFERRAL

If community isn't as easily formed or as naturally sustained as it once was, then why bother with trying to do so in business?

Here's an exercise, to be taken in your own "cone of silence," with no one monitoring you and no grades:

1. The last time you needed medical help, such as a doctor, dentist, dermatologist, optometrist, and so forth, whom did you ask outside of your family?

2. The last time you wanted information on a vacation location, whom did you ask?
3. In an upcoming decision, regarding obtaining a realtor, or accountant, or attorney on a very critical matter, whom do you intend to ask for a recommendation?
4. Think back to important recommendations you've been asked to provide (a good restaurant, a reliable airline, how to arrange an Airbnb)—who was asking you?

The reason for my little test is that, overwhelmingly, we consult with trusted peers for advice. We do not use the internet (the equivalent of the old telephone "Yellow Pages" is to Google or use Wikipedia), we do not rely on advertisements, and we don't choose to follow the advice of strangers. (The "kindness of strangers" is a lament of Blanch Dubois when she used to be a "working woman.")

This isn't anecdotal. Professor Jonah Berger of the Wharton School has been studying the phenomenon for over a decade and has written about his research.[5] His findings are that about 85 percent of executive decisions are made using peer-level references. These may be about suppliers and vendors, attractive markets, sources of talent, lobbying, and so forth.

We do the same for a wide variety of personal and professional advice, both formal and informal.

And, as you've no doubt noticed, there are entire industries and professions based on peer-level reference, for example, real estate, automotive, and insurance.

SOCIAL PROOF

When I graduated from college, I went to work for Prudential Insurance in Newark, New Jersey, the home office. About three months thereafter, my wife and I received a visit at our home from a man called Hal Mapes, who identified himself as a Prudential agent assigned to provide insurance for Prudential employees.

I told him that we had virtually no money and he said he understood, but what were my chances of advancement at Prudential if I didn't have

Prudential insurance? Besides, what if, God forbid, something happened to me or my wife?

I purchased the cheapest possible policy. I think if I died I was to be thrown off a freight train in Oklahoma.

However, three months later Hal came back, not to sell me more insurance (he evidently believed we were poor) but to get three references for him to call upon. I protested that my wife and I didn't really know anyone (we were 22), but Hal pointed out our college friends, family, neighborhood acquaintances, my wife's work colleagues, and our volunteer work.

He was asking about our various communities. We gave him three names.

Hal did this every six months. If he had 30 insureds to begin with and received 6 names from each, that's 180 names. If he closed even 10 percent of them, that's 18 new policies and now he has 48 insureds and 284 references next year.

Hal retired a very wealthy man on his commissions.

We all belong to communities, sometimes deliberately, sometimes accidentally, sometimes invisibly. But they're there with us as members.

The massive amount of auto advertising in newspapers, on television, and on other media might draw customers, but for all that investment it pales to someone telling a friend or colleague, "Go to Acme Motors, they have the best deals and their service department is a pleasure to deal with." Realtors are forever asking for listing possibilities from the acquaintances of clients.

Our unique consumer society is largely based on such referrals within communities because:

- We identify with someone who is similar to us in economic strata, profession, location, education, and/or interests.
- There is a reciprocity since we freely provide such recommendations and we're therefore confident in asking for them.
- They are far superior to trying to do elaborate research and therefore save a huge amount of time.
- There is a huge likelihood that the recommendation is based on common values and metrics so the chances of a poor choice are quite low.

However, I can't claim that these are *always* the case, because sometimes we sense a threat in making the request or following the advice.

THE MYTH OF COMPETITIVE THREAT

There is a huge irony when people become afraid of others stealing their work, ideas, intellectual property, brand, or whatever. The irony is the inverse proportion that, the more prominent the person, the less they care, the less known the person, the more the thought of theft prohibits them from entering the "public square."

I've written over 60 books, which are in 15 languages, and thousands of articles. I've spoken in videos, podcasts, and workshops, so all of my intellectual property is out there for people to embrace. Why am I unafraid of theft? For three reasons:

1. It's my IP, so no one is as good at teaching it, coaching it, and applying it as I am.
2. No one ever learned to ski by reading a book.
3. Competition doesn't narrow markets; it *broadens them.*

I'll expand on this final point by observing that Burger King, for example, builds its stores across the street from MacDonald's stores. Why? It's simple: because Burger King knows that people are going there to buy burgers.

In many cities, you'll find an intensity of certain industries and professions. When we lived in San Francisco, we would simply walk up Van Ness Street to look at every new car model in existence. Everything was there, from Volkswagen to Bentley. (Today, of course, VW *owns* Bentley!) The dealership owners knew people went to that street to consider auto purchases, so they made sure they were present.

You'll see the same in the "diamond district" in New York City on 47th and 48th streets, and "restaurant row" on West 46th between 8th and 9th Avenues. (This is regardless of economic strata. You'll find that dive bars and strip joints occupy adjacent territory as well, in most cities where they're present.)

SOCIAL PROOF

Take a look in your own city or cities you visit as to where the pizza shops, the Asian food restaurants, the pharmacies, auto repair places, and so forth are. This isn't a matter of zoning so much as a matter of *marketing*. (And, by the way, I can make a strong case that MacDonald's is in the real estate business, not the burger business.)

Thus, this myth of competitive threat is a perception that keeps us from releasing our IP and other models and approaches. We have to overcome this in order to form and sustain communities where there are mutual trust and reciprocity. Recently, a member of my global community posted a proposed table of contents for a new book he is writing on my online Forums. He then asked me whether he should take it off because it was vulnerable to others appropriating it.

"Would you take someone else's work that they posted on my Forums?" I asked.

"Of course not," he said.

"Then why think they would take yours?"

I'm not positing that all community members in all communities are scrupulously honest (think of Bernie Madoff and all those who realized that the quoted returns couldn't possibly be real), but I am confidently stating that communities have shared values, and it's unlikely that theft is one of them.

Before we depart from the competitive threat myth, I think we need to talk specifically about remote interactions: Zoom, Skype, Webex, Google Notes, and so forth.

Meetings, conversations, workshops, mastermind groups, and other variations have all migrated to what I'll collectively call (because it's the most widespread and user-friendly) Zoom. We've become "Zoom Potatoes" no less than the old "Couch Potatoes." Does this increased pajama-bottom, multitask with your email, easily recorded, and related informality add to the threat of theft and intellectual appropriation, and both advertent and inadvertent competitive theft? Yes and no.

We take advantage of the rather impressive Zoom technology[6] but often ignoring its shortcomings. Despite "rooms" there really is no substitute for live, small teamwork. And you can't control the distractions in other people's homes or offices.

However, there are steps you can take, and I advise the following to keep people fully engaged in Zoom calls and, therefore, supporting you and staying "honest":

1. Everyone must have their video on, no photo "placeholders." It's rude to others not to do so, and I want to watch people's expressions and behaviors. This is a "must"—people know the time and date and should be prepared to be seen "live."
2. Use the first 90 seconds, when people decide how much attention to provide, to intimately engage them with a story or an example or a challenge.
3. Keep Zoom presentations to no more than three hours, and include a 20-minute break within that period. Multiple, relatively brief sessions are always better.
4. Encourage people to ask questions at any time. If there's no administrator to alert you to them, ask people to simply interrupt you. This helps you calibrate your speed and efficacy.
5. Engage people with your own questions and be patient until you get a response or volunteer.

Under no circumstances should you refrain from publicizing your IP and approaches, whether alive or virtual. Let's examine now some "tools" for the community organizer.

SELF-CHECK AND SOCIAL PROOF

Here's a definition of a traditional "community organizer":

> Organizers are focused on building social organizations, expanding their membership base, raising questions or alternatives, developing sound organizing strategies, recruiting leadership, assisting with fundraising, running member meetings, and facilitating training sessions.[7]

To create your community you're going to need to take stock of yourself, your value, your beliefs, and your contributions. These need to be backed up by social proof, that is, the need to provide examples of success so that a person can adjust behavior in light of that evident success.

Your opinion isn't good enough (a huge failing of using social media to justify anything). You need to provide empirical evidence of the power and validity of your community's beliefs and values so that others can more readily "buy into" it.

We've examined earlier some of the diminished numbers within communities and the factors for those declines. The factors included issues that no longer seemed as important (diseases successfully reduced), demographic changes in potential member groups (fewer veterans), conflicting interests and distractions (extra-curricular activities and remote entertainment), and a perceived reduced value (trade associations). Figure 1.1 shows the relationship of importance and interest in communities.

Communities that have high degrees of importance and in which people have strong personal interests (e.g., the arts) feature long-term fulfillment for members. Those that have high importance but little interest for members (administration in an insurance company) represent just the daily "grind," the nine-to-five job. Those that have relatively little importance but high interest (from playing Angry Birds, to a local band, to drug use at the extreme) are addictive. And, finally, those that are neither simply create apathy and indifference (cleaning up a park, running a struggling business).

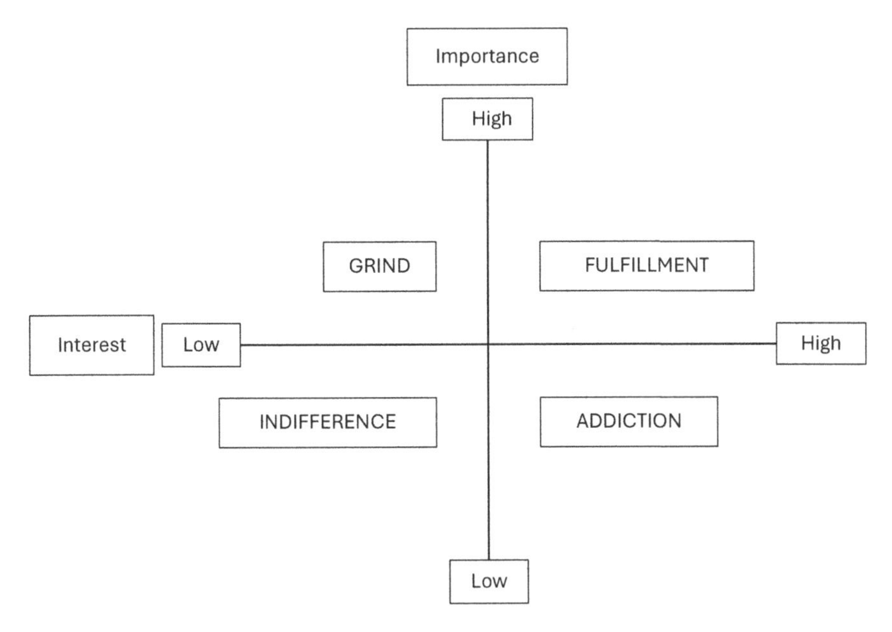

FIGURE 1.1
Importance and interest in communities.

In times of uncertainty, communities are more important than ever, yet most that form today are virtual and internet-based. There is no interpersonal aspect in terms of physical proximity, and there are unequal "givers and takers." In fact, even in the most uncontroversial and beneficent communities, it's difficult to create a spirit of "donating" one's expertise, experiences, and counsel to the community.

SOCIAL PROOF

Communities should exchange extrinsic and intrinsic knowledge. This means that what the overall community knows should be accessible to any individual within it, and that whatever an individual knows should be accessible to all others. This is nowhere so true as within business communities, so that individuals can respond to customers immediately without consulting anyone else.[8]

What are three key attributes or strengths that you have as a community organizer?

1. ______________________________
2. ______________________________
3. ______________________________

NOTES

1 Simon & Schuster, 2000.
2 See Stumbling on Happiness, Knopf, 2007.
3 concurrences.com.
4 Fox News.
5 See *Contagious,* Simon & Schuster, 2013, and *Invisible Influence,* Simon & Schuster, 2017.
6 I was interviewed recently by a global podcast using Skype. It was like returning to four-cylinder cars.
7 https://www.socialworkdegreesguide.com
8 See *The Knowledge Creating Company*, Ikujiro Sonaka and Hirotaka Takeuchi, Harvard Business School, 2008.

2

The Reality of Committees and the Fallacy of Teams

Teams share freely because all members win or lose together, hence, we're all motivated to share. But this is rarely the case. We actually work in committees, where some of us win and some of us don't win. Community can even that out and improve on an otherwise sick dynamic.

THE DEFINITIONS TELL THE STORY

We seem to be obsessed with team performance, team building, team dysfunctions, *ad nauseum*. What is a team, really? It's one or more people working together, but it's also something beyond just an informal group.

True teams win or lose together, just like an athletic team. The quarterback on a football team may have a great day, but if the other team scores more points he and his team lose. I've never heard of a game where "The Dodgers lost, but the right fielder won."

In the workplace, this means that the "R&D Team" or the "High Net Worth Investor Team," knowing they must win or lose together will:

- Share resources (budget, people, information).
- Share credit and responsibility.
- Be honest with each other.
- Present a united front.
- Support those in need (overtime, coaching).

DOI: 10.4324/9781003507321-3

At the end of the performance period, they are rewarded or not by their joint results.

And this rarely happens. Because most organizations don't have true teams, they have committees.

A committee is a group of people charged with the completion or monitoring of a specific function, comprising individuals who may or may not normally work together, and which may be temporary or permanent. "Creep" was an anacronym for "Committee to Reelect the President," which was temporary. A typical school board is a permanent committee although with changing members, whether elected or appointed.

SOCIAL PROOF

This may seem like heresy, but look around you. You hear about "Congressional committees," not "Congressional teams." We have investigative committees, and even though we have sports *teams,* we have rules *committees.*

In a committee members cooperate to the extent they are willing to do so *without jeopardizing their own self-interests.* Unlike a true team, individual committee members don't necessarily share budgets or people or information if they feel they will then be at a disadvantage having done so.

This is because *individual committee members can "win" while others "lose."* Rewards (and punishments) are applied individually, not to everyone commonly. I can win and you can lose and vice-versa on the same project.

Yet we constantly talk of "teams" even though most organizations, of all sizes, private and public, profit and nonprofit (viz. academic committees, *not teams*), are actually using committees by designation or by default!

Thus, "team building" and "team exercises" and "team experiences" aren't generally successful. I can catch you if you fall backward during a team-building exercise on some beach with the trainers looking on, smiling smugly, but back in the office, I'm not going to catch you if your error favors my advancement over yours.

What does this have to do with communities?

Communities are neither teams nor committees. They are groups which include and accommodate individuals who, as we stated at the outset, have common goals, values, and beliefs. *Within these groups both teams and committees may form, but the degree to which that happens if it happens at all has no bearing on the nature and direction of the community.*

Here's a definition of "team building" from *Oxford Languages*:

> The action or process of causing a group of people to work together effectively as a team, especially by means of activities and events designed to increase motivation and promote cooperation. Companies are starting to turn to arts-based training programs as a way of team building and improving morale.

I've never seen a method which promotes motivation and morale within a community as a blanket approach. For example, a community of small business owners participates and interacts based on their personal needs being met (as a committee member might) but also may choose to collaborate with peers on a common project which they jointly own or not (as a team member might).

"Team" and "committee" are means of organization, but "community" is a state of mind. Let's keep that in *our* minds as we evaluate our own reality.

EVALUATING YOUR OWN REALITY

I have a global community because I am primarily in the "retail" business. This means that I deal with people (probably) like you: Entrepreneurs and small business owners who seek to improve their lives through the improvement of their business.

I built my career working in the "wholesale" space, which means corporate and large organization entities, whether for-profit, nonprofit, academic, military, religious, or whatever.

These are significantly different potential communities—retail and wholesale—and you have to decide:

- In reality, what group do you want to embrace in a community?
- Why do you want to do it?
- And only then: What value will generate success?

There is also the duality of *creating a community* and *sustaining a community*. Let's examine these variables for your reality.

Write below what group(s) you wish to pursue for your community building. I've told you mine, St. Paul was pursuing potential converts to Christianity, Fedex pursues both corporate and individual shippers, and Starbucks needs people who want "designer" and somewhat aloof coffee preparation (hence, "barristas," and sizes such as "trenta" and "venti" and "Huey, Dewey, and Louie"). Note that the Dunkin' Donuts community building pursues a very different kind of coffee-drinker who probably has never tasted soy milk.

My ideal community member:

Make sure this is not overly broad. Both Starbucks and Dunkin' are dealing with coffee-drinkers, but they are very different communities. (I know you may be thinking "customers," but customers *are* communities, which is why you're reading this book. Companies from Rolls Royce to American Express, Walmart to your local hardware store, do special things for their communities.)

This leads us to my next question: Why do you want to do it? That's not the "obviousity" it appears to be. Your reasons may include:

- Increased direct business
- Increased referral business
- Laboratory for new products and services
- Legacy business
- Publicity and market share
- Improving a social condition
- Educating a profession
- Creating connection in lonely times (mental health).

These are not, of course, mutually exclusive. Write below why you seek to form a community (or improve a current one):

____

____

SOCIAL PROOF

My corporate (wholesale) communities were driven by executives who wanted to exchange marketing techniques and performance improvement options with non-competitive peers. My individual (retail) communities are driven by people who may, indeed, compete with each other, but that's unimportant compared with understanding the lifestyles and choices made by others in their positions.

This brings us to question three: How are you going to do this (what value do you provide to community members and how is it delivered to them)?

There is great value in mere connectivity. I point out to my community of hundreds of "inner circle" (frequent interaction and higher fees), thousands of "outer circle" (infrequent interaction and lower fees), and tens of thousands of "peripheral" members (rare interaction and mostly readers of my books), that to the extent they interact with each other, it's totally due to having me in common.

Thus, even when I'm not present and interacting (e.g., as I'm writing this chapter) people are interacting in person in groups we've formed, by Zoom in still other groups, on my Forums (Alansforums.com), on my private blog (Alanandthegang.com), in my newsletters, videos, podcasts, and other vehicles. They realize this, of course, but I like to remind them!

There is wonderful value in connectivity. There is also the value of my introduction of new IP (intellectual property) with regularity, both free and fee experiences (subscriptions, workshops, coaching), and other options. And then there is the value that members provide to each other, asking questions, providing answers, and doing this in the "public" of the community where everyone can benefit.

Write below the values you'll provide (we can discuss exactly how later):

____

____

____

____

____

You've now answered the three key questions for the reality of your community creation and sustainability. Be sensitive to the fact that community needs change because technology, demographics, social mores, and economies change. Just as you may have a few friends from childhood with whom you're still in contact, you've made a lot more friends as you've grown, become more successful, perhaps changed your focus, and changed your geography (not to mention your own beliefs and values).

Communities are no different, and you can maintain them through change *if you and the community are not just part of the change but are leading it in some fashion.*

INVOLVEMENT VERSUS ENTANGLEMENT

There are some communities which "entangle," meaning they are hard to escape and pose burdens, not opportunities. Cults are such communities, and the Jonestown massacre of the followers of Jim Jones in 1978, or the death of the followers of David Kourish in Waco in 1993 demonstrate the worst aspects. Some religious groups create entanglements where adherents are prohibited from leaving. When people do manage to leave, they are condemned and "forgotten." They are a disgrace to the families they leave behind.

We've all read stories about these unhealthy community connections.

Business has some similarities, in that you are expected to commit to certain behaviors that the group supports whether you choose to (or can) or not.

SOCIAL PROOF

When I was first in the corporate world I worked in a division of Prudential Insurance with 400 other employees. One day, two people came to my desk and asked that I contribute to a charity. I had little money, a small salary, and didn't particularly favor the charity, so I tried to refuse. They then told me that they'd have to report to management that I was the lone holdout preventing 100 percent division support.

I agreed to contribute the minimum amount. Later on, some veterans told me that the people asking for donations tell everyone that they're "the last holdout" when actually about 50 percent of the division actually contributed.

Normative pressure is extremely powerful but has to be used positively. For example, communities should provide:

- Voluntary membership, not mandatory membership
- Value to entice, not threats to create fear
- Pride of belonging, not embarrassment to tell others
- Individual choices of degree of participation, not dictates
- Freedom to speak with others, not a required permission
- Minimal or no dues/charges, not mandatory contributions

By an absence of "entanglement," I also mean a freedom to come and go and a lack of censure (assuming you behave respectfully and observe reasonable rules of conduct). I belonged to a virtual community of Lionel Train enthusiasts who would show pictures of their layouts, buy and sell items, share techniques for wiring and scenery, and so forth. It was highly beneficial, free, and of high value.

But the administrators had to shut down all comments and eventually freeze the site because people engaged in political name-calling, obscene comments, and boorish behavior—on a model train site!

You shouldn't feel that you have to compete in a community, nor participate to any arbitrary degree. I've never minded "lurkers" who simply read or listen but don't choose to proactively participate. That's up to the individual. But I also prohibit "drive-by bragging," where someone shows up only on the occasion to boast about some accomplishment and award.

Let's understand that community is based not on self-aggrandizement but rather on self-effacing behavior. That may sound strange, but I'm referring to our willingness to share defeats, setbacks, and errors so that (1) others can learn from them, and (2) we can learn ways to prevent the same issues in the future. We don't grow by merely focusing on success; we grow by learning from setbacks and preventing them from recurring.

The people who don't grow are those who don't admit to defeat and try to preserve their weak egos, instead of using strong egos to welcome solicited feedback. (And that's why strong people always welcome coaches, because they know they can always improve and aren't afraid to admit it, while weak people avoid coaches because admitting that they need one they see as an indication of weakness.)

I often refer to the "Lobster Principle" with my clients. No one knows for sure how long lobsters live, or how big they can become. An 80-pound creature was caught and, thankfully, released, and one believed to be 100 years was also found. (A kind of clam called a Quahog, which loves cold waters, was found in the Arctic, and its rings indicated it was 500 years old. The oldest known land animal, the giant tortoise, has one member determined to be 193 at this writing.)

Lobsters have an exoskeleton, which we call a "shell." Since the skeleton doesn't grow as the lobster grows inside of it, the lobster "molts," which means it sheds its shell while the new one is forming. During that period it hides from predators because it's vulnerable.

We, too, have to be vulnerable in order to grow. There are no predators seeking us out if we are mentally and emotionally healthy. *Hence, a community serving its members well will be a safe place for such vulnerability, during which people can grow and improve.* People don't grow by merely defending themselves.

WHY WE LIE TO OURSELVES ABOUT COLLABORATION

We live in a competitive world, which can often be tough and draining. After all, capitalism is based on competition to make the best products and provide the best services at varying price points with sufficient profit to enable the provider to stay in business, hire employees, and invest in the future.

There is also the informal competition caused by the mass traditional media and the more recent social media. We see mansions, luxury cars, fine clothes, fancy restaurants, and other manifestations of a great (materialistic) life. We aspire to be a part of it in most cases. But even on a more localized level, we watch our kids' sports teams compete and root vociferously, we may try to beat another driver to a merge, we want the best seat in a popular restaurant, and we seek upgrades wherever we can get them. (We recently attended a Broadway play that had a "VIP room" for guests willing to pay a few extra dollars to avoid the lines and obtain some free refreshments.)

It's easy to form a community around your son or daughter's soccer team, but not so much with the entire league's parents because you're competing with them regularly. I know, you're thinking of professional athletes who routinely congratulate the other team after the game, win or lose. But you're probably also familiar with the violence among parents at high school and municipal sports events, with ejections and sometimes arrests.

SOCIAL PROOF

It's more and more difficult in Canada and the US to enlist officials for community sports because the abuse from parents is often overwhelming and boils over into threats and physical assault. The games are even worse when the lack of volunteers results in fewer and/or poorer officials.[1]

We talk about "collaboration" but it's often a lie (or a misunderstanding) for the same reason that a committee is not a team. We're willing to collaborate until it comes down to personal sacrifice. We may be best of friends within our kid's hockey team, but we're each going to pull for our kid to get the starting job and be upset if it goes to another parent's child, even if we engage in fund-raisers together.

In fact, "collaborator" has often had a very pejorative connotation. "Collaborator" is often applied by prevailing powers to label those believed to be in opposition to it, working for "the enemy." During the "Red Scare" and blacklisting in the US over fears of Communism, members of that party and those who aided and abetted them were often deemed to be "collaborators." Of two definitions in the dictionary, one specifically cites "collaboration" as "working with an enemy" and "traitorous."[2]

Collaboration, in its positive sense, seems far more appropriate for use with committees.

In communities we neither focus on committees nor teams, but rather members. But what are the requirements for membership? We stated at the outset that these were different from "tribes."

Communities have their own cultures. "Culture" is another term that's rather carelessly thrown around. I'm defining it here for you and for our purposes:

Culture is that set of beliefs which governs behavior

Simple as that. So within our community, which I've stipulated has shared beliefs, we operate in accordance with them.

If you remember Enron, it had a belief system of defrauding customers. True communities have an internal mechanism for discovering and dealing with behaviors not consistent with the prevailing community beliefs. A normal reaction would be, in order of less to more severity:

- Critique by peers
- Formal complaints to community leaders
- Penalties such as limited access or reduction of benefits
- Expulsion

People have experienced this in religious communities (defrocking, excommunication), legal communities (disbarment), government (censure, impeachment), business (demotion, transfer, termination), sports (trades, releases), medicine (review committees, privileges suspended), and entertainment (refusals to hire). This is sometimes readily done and sometimes only done under great pressure.

The #metoo movement resulted in long overdue action against Harvey Weinstein, Jeffrey Epstein, Bill Cosby, Matt Lauer, Charlie Rose, and a host of others. But they were protected for a long time within their respective communities by managers, agents, co-workers, and producers who either shared the poor ethical behavior or were simply too scared for their jobs to raise the problem to authorities.

Those "beliefs which govern behavior" can be salutary or disgraceful, but they nonetheless *do* govern members' behaviors.

Within a healthy community there are commonly accepted, observed, and manifest behaviors which reflect a mutual belief system. And they are the means to create true connectivity, to which we'll now turn.

NOTES

1 In a famous psychological study, the loyal customers of Dunkin' and Starbucks were given free coffee for a month to see how many would "desert" to the other provider. After the test period, the results were . . . ZERO! Dunkin' people thought Starbucks was like invading someone's living room and had too many bizarre choices. Starbucks' customers couldn't believe the lack of couches and so few coffee options. https://www.chegg.com/homework-help/questions-and-answers/real-maretngw2-earthlings-says-executive-dunkins-ad-agency-starbucks-customers-dunkin-paid-q26137444

2 *New Oxford American Dictionary.* USA Today, https://www.usatoday.com/story/sports/2023/10/15/parent-behavior-in-youth-sports-is-abusive-officials-dont-feel-safe/71194511007/

3

The Inordinate Power of Connectivity

There's nothing new about networking and making introductions, but there's a great deal new in formalizing those dynamics and turning them into a unique value.

NONE OF YOU WOULD KNOW EACH OTHER WITHOUT ME

I'm an inveterate, eclectic collector: postage stamps, model trains, cigars, fine wine, match books, and hotel stationery. It may be eccentric, but I'm not bothering anyone or shoplifting. They are harmless hobbies.

One of the things I collect are rocks. I'll find one in a country we're visiting, write the location on the rock, and take it home. They all fit in the palm of my hand, the customs officials don't care, and I place them around my den. So, as I type these works, they are on shelves and credenzas all around me, perhaps a hundred or more. I've been to over 60 countries and often collect from different cities and parts of a country (e.g., Beijing and Hong Kong).

I have rocks from a safari in South Africa, near the Great Wall, an Australian game preserve, the moonscape of the Icelandic countryside, and the island of Mykonos. Most recently I brought back a mineral-laden rock from the Mendenhall Glacier, where we landed in a helicopter.

One day sitting here, writing a prior book for my publisher, I looked around seeking some ideas for a point I was attempting to make. I took joy, as I always do, looking at the rocks spread around and I said (and I'm always sober when I write), "You know, none of you would know each other without me!"

DOI: 10.4324/9781003507321-4

The rocks didn't respond, but my prefrontal cortex did: None of the people in my community would know each other without me as the common factor. (It's actually about 99.8 percent since some people introduced friends and colleagues to me.)

SOCIAL PROOF

Uber-coach, Marshall Goldsmith, my friend and collaborator on *Lifestorming,* was speaking at one of my events and was asked how to become a thought leader. He said, "Hang out with them," and told us how he had—literally—carried the great Peter Drucker's briefcase for him to meetings and events.

I began thinking more diligently about what is "connectivity" worth. After all, I pioneered value-based fees in consulting back in the 1990s.[1] What is the value of people interacting in person and remotely, with or without my presence, globally? Here's what it is for my community and what it would be for yours:

- A relief from feeling isolated in one company or one profession, especially for those working remotely and alone. (That wasn't a factor as much when my community began 25 years ago.)
- Meeting those "kindred spirits" who can immediately relate to one's situation and circumstances.
- Finding solutions, innovation, and new approaches to common issues and challenges.
- Carrying communication "off-line" so that you can form collegial relationships with a few people at a time. (Not everything needs to be "public" in larger groups.)
- Making true friends. (Although not common, this has occasionally led to serious personal relationships.)
- Making contributions to others, which builds one's esteem and sense of worth.
- Understanding global issues from true sources, not the internet or other secondary sources. (American media often resemble a child's game of "telegraph," distorting foreign events which I've found clarified by talking to local people.)

- Dealing with personal issues via anonymous community provisions, learning from people who have been through them. (And, on occasion, people have come to me privately and personally, and I've wound up helping six people through divorces and a dozen through personal loss.)
- Learning of opportunities in the same professions, markets, and industries, and of opportunities appropriate in new professions, markets, and industries. (Many executives prepare to be consultants when they retire, for example.)

As I'm writing this, people from all over the world are:

- Interacting on my online platform[2]
- Utilizing my online remote learning programs[3]
- Communicating with each other via Zoom, email, Instagram, phone, and other media, as well as following each other on social media platforms
- Collaborating on projects and/or meeting each other for social and business conversations

Post-pandemic, more than ever, "communities" are essential vehicles for camaraderie and companionship and collegiality. You may not yet have formed one or, as was my case, may have one and not realize it, with the opportunity to formalize it. I've done this with both corporate and individual (entrepreneurial) community members.

Let's turn to how you can create a "critical mass" of members at the outset. (We'll cover this in greater detail and tactics in the next chapter.)

ST. PAUL WAS THE FIRST VIRAL MARKETER

St. Paul was virulently anti-Christian until his epiphany on the road to Damascus. After that, he became the leading advocate and Apostle, even more so than Peter, who would become the first Pope. If not for the voluminous writings of Paul, we'd know far less about those times and virtually nothing about Jesus, who, of course, left no writings of his own.

Paul traveled to Corinth, Rome, Athens, Thessalonica, Berea, Neopolis, Samothrace, Amphpolis, Ephesus, Caesarea, and Antioch. He may have covered as much as 10,000 miles on land and sea over 30 years. At each of these locations he would explain the tenets and advantages of Christian belief, and he would urge all those present to go tell other people, to spread the word.

Christians accounted for approximately 10 percent of thc Roman population by300, according to some estimates. Christianity then rapidly grew in the fourth century, accounting for 56.5 percent of the Roman population by350. That growth astounds some modern statisticians.

Paul was the first viral marketer.

Communities require viral marketing. We don't need to trek around a half-dozen countries like Paul, and we have the benefit of mass, global communications. However, we do need his zeal and commitment.

We discussed earlier the Christian communities of his time providing support and succor for others. This was immensely appealing in an age when people led hardscrabble, treacherous, and short lives. In these far easier (but sometimes no less daunting) times, potential community members need a different kind of support.

They need emotional support, mental support, and intellectual support, and sometimes material support. Let me briefly explain the differences.

Emotional Support: Logic helps people to think, but emotions enable them to act. When you seek to have consumers buy a competitive product, it's important to create an emotional bond (brands often do this: people feel good about driving a Bentley or wearing Brioni clothing), but it's important to control emotions as well; otherwise, we have "road rage" (and what I've coined as "life rage").

Mental Support: Great ideas and novel solutions and innovation are generated by interacting frequently with thought leaders. This is *not* the "skunk works" approach of putting supposedly creative people in a room, throwing them some red meat, and locking the doors. It's about the frequency of exchanging views until the right combination of passion, insight, and novelty is annealed. (This is how scientists account for life forming: certain cells, acids, minerals, and whatever coming together in a huge accident over millions of years.) You can't simply attend a workshop or, even more unlikely, read a book. You need to interact regularly.

Intellectual Support: I've separated this from "mental support" because this is about "learning how to learn." Mental support is about the content of new ideas and thinking, but intellectual support is about the *process* of becoming a "perpetual learning machine." Most college students today learn irrelevancies that can be easily looked up later using AI. But they don't learn how to learn so they're active learning ends after school because the content becomes obsolete and the *process was never learned and mastered.*

Material Support: In a community, people learn of physical means they don't have, or they have and are not appropriate. For example, certain equipment is needed for an effective Zoom meeting *and there's also a need not to go overboard with equipment.* The same holds true of computers, printers, cell phones, copiers, and so on. For example, having listened to others, I made sure my computers had a "touch" feature to remember and apply passwords. There are also services in this category, such as tax work, subcontractors, technical people, financial advisors, publicity sources, and so forth. The greatest source of reliable advice is peer-to-peer referral, as we've mentioned previously.

SOCIAL PROOF

In my communities people exchange advice and experiences on everything from writing implements, computers, and important club memberships to vacation spots, legal assistance, and restaurants.

This is the "viral help" that communities provide with or without your personal intervention, but always with your credit for having brought people together.

THE POST-PANDEMIC BLUES

The pandemic is a milestone event. Even if the medical effects have been ameliorated (which is debatable), the social impact is huge and continuing. Some of the evidence:

- Some people continue to wear masks, which also serves as a "warning" to others and is an extreme behavior if one isn't otherwise medically compromised. Covid transmission interpersonally would require

someone in very close proximity for an extended period of time. Also, masks prompt people to keep touching their faces, which can cause further disease spread.
- "Live" business meetings have been hugely reduced, from conventions of thousands to conferences among a few people.[4]
- Business travel has been commensurately reduced with remote meetings preferred.
- People are suffering from mental health issues being in isolation in their homes, even with family, because of the inability to have lunch or a drink with co-workers.
- Work pressures have mounted as leaders try to figure out how to assign and measure productivity among people who are not physically present. This has ranged from many tech workers never coming into an office to Elon Musk demanding that his SpaceX workers show up physically for 40 hours a week.

People are more isolated than ever, and more despairing than ever. Add to the increasing automation and AI integration and the trend worsens. Once upon a time a driver could chat with a gas station attendant about politics, sports, the weather, and so forth. Now, most gas stations are self-serve, attached to a mini-mart. (The gas pump, however, does talk to you, since it's programmed to play advertisements.)[5]

High self-esteem is required for consistently high performance and it is far harder to maintain in isolation. Figure 3.1 positions two key factors.

When efficacy (how well you do things) and esteem (your feelings of self-worth) are both high, you tend to perform better and are more resilient when facing a setback. When self-esteem is low yet efficacy is high, you feel like an imposter. (An actor with an award gained for portraying someone else will tend to worry if he or she will ever work again.)

When esteem is high but efficacy is not, we have the "empty suit" who talks a good game but doesn't deliver. And when both are low we have disaffected people. The French word "anomie" lends itself to anomic suicide, an extreme reaction to disaffection.

We've made some progress in dealing with business needs and travel needs since the pandemic, with supply chains and international trade, but not so much with emotional needs. Our ability to express ourselves to colleagues and acquaintances, to learn whether our positions are supported or resisted, and to share a laugh or a celebration are severely reduced.

Self-Esteem

Efficacy	HIGH	LOW
HIGH	Health	"Imposter"
LOW	"Empty Suit"	Disaffection ("Anomie")

FIGURE 3.1
Maintaining high self-esteem.

It's true that people continue to gather in large numbers for sports and entertainment events, whether locally or remotely, but these aren't frequent and far from intimate. A million people might gather for New Year's in Times Square, but they're only sharing some moments in time and not personal sentiments. (Is there anything so superficial as an entertainer telling the audience that he or she "loves them all"?)

We've actually made more emotional progress, however, socially than we have professionally and in business settings. Coffee shops are still jammed in the mornings, restaurants are overflowing, some golf courses and pickleball courts are filled. Most people in these venues know each other and continue the relationship, and newcomers are usually welcomed.

But in business we don't enjoy equal opportunities. There are three huge problems:

1. You can't casually continue relationships. There is no cubicle next door and you can't expect just to contact someone on Facetime or Zoom. There are no chance meetings in the halls, restrooms, or elevators. There's no common coffee area in which to complain about the coffee.
2. You can't network. Prospects, suppliers, peers, and customers are not around. On a remote basis you can't single them out and go for a drink or lunch. It's very hard to develop relationships remotely (exacerbated by people who refuse to turn on their video, as we've discussed earlier).

3. The distractions are far more severe. On site you're not likely to pick up a guitar and try to play a diminishing fifth, or get to Level 20 on Angry Birds, or try on a new outfit, or watch Celebrity Family Feud, or replay an athletic event you taped. Nor are your kids going to ask for help with a toy, nor your dog demand you both take a walk (sometimes indicating an accident might take place in your presence). A non-working spouse (yes, there are still plenty of them) thinks nothing of walking in to discuss dinner because "you're not really working."

These are blues that can be ameliorated when you form effective communities (which we'll demonstrate in the next chapter). There are reports of leaders being less inclined to promote people whom they don't frequently see in person (or at all).

SOCIAL PROOF

Nothing startles someone working at home as much as a call from the boss that's unexpected and requests the person immediately get on Zoom or Facetime for an important issue. At the office you're not worried about what you're wearing, if you have makeup on, or if you've combed your hair, because you arrived "presentable."

ACCRUING VALUE WHILE YOU EAT, SLEEP, TRAVEL, AND MAKE MERRY

We'll conclude this first part of the book on the nature, reasons for, and purposes of community in this section before venturing into the actual implementation. Thus, we've been talking about "why" and "what" and not yet "how."

We've also been talking largely about the value for members, since that's the selling point and sustaining factor. Some of that value is apparent, something members want and even crave, and some of that value is non-apparent, something they need but don't realize.

It's incumbent upon you to address the "wants" but even more importantly to establish the "needs." *Ironically, perhaps, that same dynamic applies to you!*

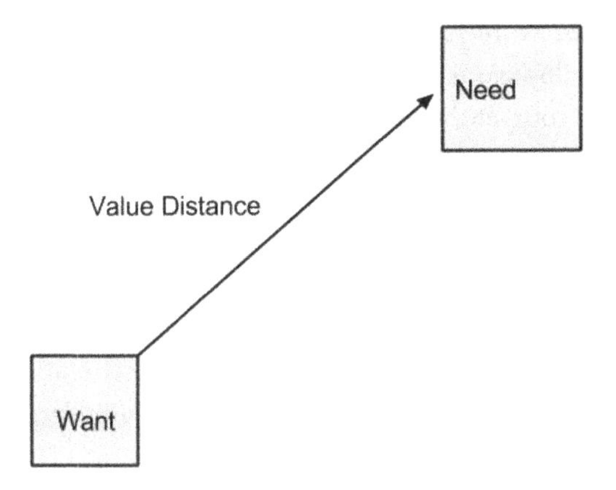

FIGURE 3.2
Want versus need.

In Figure 3.2, you'll see what I term the "value distance" that emerges between what people perceive they want and what is demonstrated as what they actually need:

That "value distance" is what people are willing to pay for in terms of investing money, but even more importantly, time. If that distance is just a few centimeters in perceptions, it's not worth much. But if it's perceived as miles, it's worth a great deal.

This is no exaggeration. Have you ever read a book, attended a performance, or joined an association which you felt greatly enriched you, perhaps more than you ever anticipated? These are the entities for which you'll continue your engagement (the author, the theater, the chapter, and so forth) without much vacillation at all. The value is overwhelming.

SOCIAL PROOF

When you receive those subscription notices from a publication (usually months in advance) or renewal notices from a club or association, do you sometimes debate whether or not to continue? We all do at some point with some offers. What we're considering while we evaluate is whether to continue the investment in terms of the perceived value received. *And there are times when we say "enough" and drop out.*

That value *must be there for you as the community organizer.* Otherwise, you're going to allow your role as founder and "chief propellant officer" to attenuate. Once your enthusiasm wanes, so will everyone else's, and with lightning speed. So it's important to understand exactly what's in it for you, not merely as the founder but also as the sustainer:

- A laboratory to try out new ideas and approaches with a diversity of potential buyers and recommenders, with minimum investment
- The creation of such IP and innovative ideas as you work with community members, helping them to solve their problems and overcome their challenges
- Passive income which will be created by the viral impact of people talking to each other, not solely within the community *but also outside of it.* Remember St. Paul, the first viral marketer? These are your evangelists.
- The credit for people's improvement whether you intervened directly or merely provided the means for others to help their peers without your direct involvement
- The ability to develop a truly global brand should you decide to establish a worldwide membership
- Case studies provided by members which you can use with their permission in your marketing
- Participation in your independent marketing and promotion with community members' testimonials, endorsements, and name recognition
- The ability to "stagger" generations, so that as people retire or move or change positions, you'll have others who take their places
- Direct sales opportunities with advantages and discounts for community members
- Promotion for your new offerings, books, and events, and so forth, both from formal endorsement and peer-level referral[6]

As you can see, the value of community is enormous, both actively and passively, directly intervening and just sitting back. The community operates "in the background" whether you're present, on an assignment, on vacation, dealing with personal issues, or whatever.

Here are some considerations for underscoring and sustaining the value of "connectivity" and community without your actual engagement on a large scale:

1. Attract people with their own informal (or even formal) communities, people who are "influencers" in the old sense (i.e., known for their success and ideas, not merely social media personalities). They will attract in turn their followers and admirers. I call this "the chain reaction of attraction"®.
2. Provide a diverse offering of in-person sessions, remote sessions, podcasts, videos, online platforms, newsletters, blog posts, and so forth. Some people will be attracted to the wide variety and others to just one avenue. You never know.
3. Accommodate a global audience. For example, record what you do so that people who can't attend in person can access the recording. Occasionally, have events at 7 am or 7 pm to accommodate people overseas. (I like to run 90-minute, remote programs at 10:00 am US eastern time, which isn't too early for the west coast, and also can accommodate Europe.)
4. Keep contemporary issues in front of your audience, not just theory. Instigate discussion about real-world, real-time events which affect your community members, which they can relate to as relevant. (That's why I've named the "call-out" boxes in these chapters "social proof.")
5. Accept the "lurking" of some people who don't actively contribute. Don't insist that people contribute and, similarly, prohibit people from bragging and only talking about themselves and their accomplishments.
6. Accept departures. People have their good reasons. Don't take this personally. Just make sure that your new "recruits" outnumber your departures!

VIGNETTE

I was speaking to a group of about 40 people on behalf of a client. I noticed a woman in the back row knitting continually and never looking up and never asking a question. I was surprised to find her waiting in line to speak with me when I had finished.

When it was her turn she asked a highly insightful question about my presentation.

"You look surprised," she said.

"Frankly," I replied, "I saw you knitting and thought you weren't paying attention."

"The knitting helps me to focus," she explained.

Everyone has their own style of learning, and you have to be tolerant and supportive of that in your community.

What are the primary values for you to acquire/achieve in your community?

1. ______________________________
2. ______________________________
3. ______________________________

Let's examine now how to specifically form your community.

NOTES

1 *Value Based Fees,* John Wiley & Sons, third edition, 2021.

2 https//www.alansforums.com

3 https://alanweiss.com/growth-experiences/

4 Office Meetings Before & After the Pandemic https://www.linkedin.com/pulse/office-meetings-before-after-pandemic-tamojit-saha/

5 New Jersey, where I grew up, has an inordinate fear of citizens self-immolating and has made self-service illegal. So you can talk sports to the attendant in Jersey—if the attendant speaks English.

6 When one of my new books is released, I offer community members a free seat in a Zoom workshop on the topic *if* they buy the book and feel it merits a five-star review on Amazon.

Part Two

Creating A Community

4

The Seven Essential Steps of Community Building

Premise: I've been able to codify this so that people learn it in person, virtually, and even independently. It's a process that can readily be mastered and applied. That's rare for "self-help." You may have already completed some of these steps, deliberately or accidentally. But even if you've done none of them, this sequence will enable you to formally create a community in as little as 90 days.

A COMMON EXPERIENCE

Just as one of the primary factors of the growth of the early Church was a common experience,[1] there has to be a common experience—or set of experiences—for your community.

This requires a global perspective ("catholic" actually means "universal"). You can't be local, regional, or even national. Not only do you want to appeal to global interests eventually if not immediately, but within the US we're dealing with a wide diversity of ethnicities, backgrounds, and even cultures.

So the first step is to have a very broad appeal, whether you're dealing with manufacturing managers, financial executives, engineers, entrepreneurs—whoever constitutes your community. Examine the issues of the times and the anticipated issues. No one predicted the internet, nor the pandemic, but we can predict demographic shifts (morbidity outpacing fertility), technology changes (ChatGPT and AI), social mores changes (social justice demands, climate concerns), and so forth.

DOI: 10.4324/9781003507321-6

Don't look at your proposed demographic (membership) strictly in terms of business or profession but in terms of "one life" that encompasses all the aspects of their lives. Hence, you want to encourage (healthy) political, economic, social, relationship, financial, and similar issues. We are more than our jobs, *and a community has to be inclusive of all the factors influencing our lives and work.*

Write down five issues that you think are, or will be, of significant importance and interest to your community members:

1. ______________________________
2. ______________________________
3. ______________________________
4. ______________________________
5. ______________________________

IMPROVED CONDITIONS FOR MEMBERS

Now that you've prepared your basic environment in terms of the issues of importance, let's examine the actual results important for your members, bearing in mind our drill and hole metaphor from earlier.

Don't be premature in terms of *how* people will interact, but rather *what* will be the return on their investment of time and money (the latter only if you charge for membership). What will people gain *that they wouldn't gain otherwise without being with you and with their peers—the connectivity?*

Put yourself in their position. It seems obvious that people would like to make more money, achieve higher status and repute, and achieve business growth. Think about:

- Improved discretionary time
- Increased referrals and new clients
- Greater and more efficient use of technology
- Opportunities unknown or unappreciated that are learned
- Metrics created for aspirations
- Personal needs met (ideal colleges, vacation spots, etc.)
- Questions answered "external" to one's business
- Opportunities to celebrate and to "mourn"

These are just some of the improved conditions, generically, that would make your community worthwhile. They need to be promoted because they account for three important goals:

1. Attraction of members
2. Retention of members
3. Recruiting of new members by existing members (evangelism)

Write down five improved conditions that you think are, or will be, of significant importance and interest to your specific community members:

1. ______________________________
2. ______________________________
3. ______________________________
4. ______________________________
5. ______________________________

SOCIAL PROOF

You've probably belonged to dozens of formal or informal communities during your life. You abandoned some, tolerated others you thought were mandatory for your career, and enjoyed and happily participated in others. The differences were in the improved conditions you found or didn't find in each.

CHALLENGES AND ENJOYMENT FOR MEMBERS

Have you ever met people who read solely business books? They think they're educating themselves but they're kidding themselves. True education derives from a wide variety of input, including diverse reading.

I learn a great deal from fiction, from games, from travel, from trying new food. I'm sure you do, as well. Therefore, your community has to provide options for learning, growth, and, not surprisingly, entertainment.

Within your community, via electronic platforms, live events, remote events, and varied media (audio, video, Zoom, and so forth) you can offer:

- Competitive games (trivia contests)
- Visual humor (cartoons)

- Challenges (case studies)
- Education (discussion of current events)
- Exploration (sharing vacation highlights)
- External opinions (editorials)

A community cannot sustain itself merely on discussions of business, profit, and growth. It is not an MBA extension program. (And in most MBA programs, the students are barely taught anything about managing and leading people.)

Write down five education/entertainment/experiential options that you think are, or will be, of significant importance and interest to your specific community members:

1. ______________________________
2. ______________________________
3. ______________________________
4. ______________________________
5. ______________________________

INTRODUCTIONS TO OTHERS IN A SUPPORT SYSTEM

The value of "none of you would know each other without me" intrinsically considers the probability that community members would *want to know each other!* You have to demonstrate the value of such collegiality early on (as time goes by, it becomes self-evident).

People are able to interact via:

- Your online platforms, operating 24/7
- Letters to your publications which you print
- Guest columns you post on your blog
- Live events you run and/or host
- Remote events you run and/or host
- Awards and recognition[2]
- Competitive games
- Participation in case studies

- Opportunities to collaborate on projects
- Small group live and remote meetings without you
- Opportunities to "brag" about business results
- Sharing of IP
- Joint problem-solving opportunities
- Time shifting (or repeating) some meetings in varying time zones

Once these opportunities are introduced, they become self-perpetuating as people find their best partners and collaborators. I also believe in healthy disagreements (without *ad hominem* attacks) to keep people on their toes and to gain respect for "pushing back."

Write down five techniques you'd use to maximize members' opportunities to meet each other and interact:

1. ______________________________
2. ______________________________
3. ______________________________
4. ______________________________
5. ______________________________

RESOLUTIONS FOR CHRONIC AND TEMPORARY PROBLEMS

We'll turn now to pragmatic and immediate help which tends to accelerate the pace at which people involve themselves and urge others to do so. I've often thought of the community as a "teaching hospital" where you learn, watch, apply, and receive feedback.

I consider myself the chief of staff!

SOCIAL PROOF

People in a vibrant community both "give and take." They provide advice and seek advice. For example, people in my community were asking what to do when a major proposal was rejected and a competitor chosen. The powerful advice: Ask the prospect, "What could I have done better to have earned your business?" That will help your success in the future.

If you have a variety of avenues to communicate and a variety of topics that can be addressed, people will find the community a place for reasonable and respectable political debate, a source for improving business practices and models, and even compassionate discussions about family and relationships.

Although I have a Ph.D. in psychology, I'm not a clinician, but we do have clinicians in the community. And we have anonymous access where the person seeking help is not identified. We've helped people through divorces, family trauma, loss of loved ones, loss of pets, downturns in finances, and so forth. This is best done with people who have "been there and done that" instead of theoretical (or even therapeutic) help.

This is the reality of our times, which too many people feel forces them to endure these hardships alone. Don't think of community as solely business-oriented because we don't have a "business life" and a "personal life."

We simply have a life, and "life balance" is about blending the two not trying to run them concurrently.

Nothing unravels careers and professions so much as money problems and relationship problems, and those two factors are inextricably intertwined. Thus, community is about a holistic approach to one's being, not merely a compartment of division of it.

Write down five access points and interactive devices you'd use to address such problem areas:

1. ____________________
2. ____________________
3. ____________________
4. ____________________
5. ____________________

THE EMPIRICAL EVIDENCE FOR AN IMPROVED FUTURE

One of the most dramatic and attractive features of a community isn't merely the promise of growth and an improved future *but the evidence of such improvement.* While bragging is unacceptable, candid explanations of success should be encouraged and welcomed.

The relevancy of a peer succeeding can't be overemphasized. And people who are successful generally love to explain their techniques and practices. (If people didn't wish to share and participate, they usually wouldn't join communities.)

This also allows you, as the community host, to talk about successes without seeming self-aggrandizing.

Here's what I mean by "empirical evidence":

1. It's based on a current prospect or client encounter or project. It is neither theoretical nor "historical."
2. It's personal, not the relating of someone else's experience.
3. The "loop can be closed" if it's an ongoing encounter.
4. People are vulnerable. That is, they ask for advice, admit to errors, and don't posture as being perfect and infallible.
5. With discretion, names are used. No one says, "I was working with a major bank . . . ." Individual names may be withheld but institutions are cited, private and public.
6. The advice and practices noted are repeatable and generic. That is, someone isn't successful because their uncle Louie is the client's president.
7. Special circumstances aren't required. That is, one needn't be a professional engineer (PE) or have a Ph.D. in Latin American politics or speak French.

As people begin to share their experiences with evidence and facts, others will be able to adapt, develop, and apply the skills necessary. This makes your community—whether this is done live, remotely, or in combination—a unique and invaluable resource.

Write down five experiences that you've had, positive and negative, that you would share as empirical evidence in your community:

1. ______________________________
2. ______________________________
3. ______________________________
4. ______________________________
5. ______________________________

SALUTARY EXPERIENCES (PLACES, DEBATES, LEARNING)

You need to attract people at first, of course (and in the next chapter we'll talk about how to do that at launch) but after that they have to want to be there. You can't try to cajole them daily, and people don't have the same kind of reactions to enticements in any case.

So, "they gotta wanna."

This means that the experience of attending community events and offerings is positive and rewarding. Having contests, games, humor, theater reviews, vacation tips, car recommendations, and so forth should be considered. I've realized that allowing a forum for political, religious, and even sexual debates and points of view makes the community more interesting and participative. I enforce rules about polite behavior and I stop all debates that become rancorous (which are rare).

How far can you go? I even have an online forum board that is titled "Sex, Religion, and Politics."

At first I thought my community should focus exclusively on business improvement. But I watched and didn't interfere as it turned into a "salon" where people could talk to true peers about whatever is on their minds, *which actually does increase their business.*

Our technology includes an option for people to immediately see what's been posted on my online platform since their last visit, and even to be notified when new comments are posted.

This is an age of loneliness, even for those showing up at the office regularly. The opportunity to have someone to talk to is huge.

SOCIAL PROOF

Some people craved such personal, intimate help that I began an offering called "The Den," which was a 90-day, one-on-one experience covering personal and family issues.

Write down five experiences you'll consider, live or remote, to entice people to voluntarily keep returning your community events and offerings:

1. ______________________________
2. ______________________________
3. ______________________________

4. ______________________________
5. ______________________________

NOTES

1 And even today, wherever you go in the world and whatever language is spoken, the Catholic Mass is the same.

2 For example, see my Million Dollar Consulting® Hall of Fame: https://alanweiss.com/growth-experiences/million-dollar-consulting-hall-of-fame/

5

The Keys to a Successful Launch

We will talk now about overcoming inertia and beginning your community. Some people have accomplished this in weeks, not months, some never, and some only had to be made aware that one already exists! Follow this sequence to maximize your chances of success.

WHO ARE YOUR IDEAL MEMBERS?

The first question is easy: You're either in the wholesale (corporate and SME) market or in the retail (solo practitioners and entrepreneurs) market. (If you feel you're in both markets, you'll need two communities, so decide with which to begin.)

It's more difficult (I didn't say "impossible," I said "difficult") to form communities in the wholesale market because corporate executives don't have the same amount of discretionary time that entrepreneurs have, and business owners are usually extremely busy. But these are far from insurmountable issues, because the empirical evidence shows there are over 40,000 trade associations in the US, and firms such as MacKay CEO Forums, Vistage, and others catering to workshops and communities for small business owners (as so chambers of commerce and service clubs).

There is a precedent for joining colleagues in both "camps." That's the good news. The bad news is that you have to stand out in this crowd.

That means that your "ideal member" has to be fairly narrowly defined, at least at the outset. See Figure 5.1 for a dispersal of potential members.

We want those people typically called "early adapters." I've termed them here "hang-tens" (extreme right) representing surfers who are highly

DOI: 10.4324/9781003507321-7

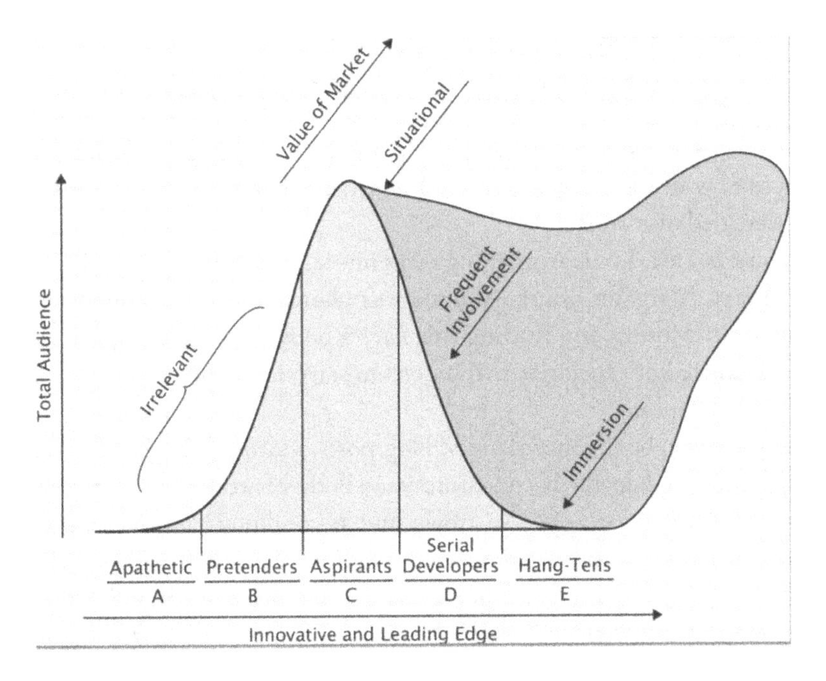

FIGURE 5.1
Ideal initial members.

innovative in their moves by hanging their toes off the front edge of the board. Note that this is not a traditional bell curve in that I've given it depth.

You're better off with a limited potential of highly likely candidates than a huge potential of unlikely candidates: the apathetic, pretenders, aspirants, and serial developers in the illustration.

You may decide on manufacturing plant managers, financial consultants, medical office staff, trademark attorneys, or sales directors. On the corporate side you won't get CEOs but you can get business owners. (I don't consider these two positions the same, though many people use them interchangeably which undermines their marketing efforts.) On the retail side you *will* be able to attract solo practitioners of a wide variety of revenue levels.

It's up to you to decide this: *Who (what positions) do I most want to attract for whom I can provide value and sustain their membership and recruitment of others?* This will depend on your value and body of work, but we'll get to that in a minute.

Whom do you wish to attract to your community by job title?

WHAT "BODY OF WORK" IS YOUR FOUNDATION?

A "body of work" is the existing (and often planned) aggregate of someone's production, which is often literary and/or artistic, but can be any consistent subject tackled over time.

Picasso's was art, Louis Armstrong's was music, Jimmy Breslin's was sports commentary, Margaret Bourke-White's was photography, and mine is consulting skills. Most of you reading this *have* a body of work, though it may not be organized or categorized. You need to start doing this, pulling things together, so to speak.

Your podcasts, books, newsletters, blog posts, videos, workshops, coaching, speeches, and so forth constitute your body of work. It has probably changed over the years as you've grown and as conditions around you have changed. (Imagine a body of work on communications that doesn't include the internet or commentary on sports that doesn't include Caitlan Clark.)

The body of work will be what *attracts and retains community members.* Therefore, you have to formalize it. Categories that are too broad don't usually work. Armstrong, mentioned prior, has a body of work around jazz, but Vivaldi, also a musician, has a body of work around classical Baroque music. Breslin covered all sports, but Vince Scully focused only on broadcasting the Dodgers baseball team for 67 years.

A body of work never "ends" in terms of constant additions and surviving retirement, disability, and even death. People still listen to Sinatra, learn from Drucker, and read Dickens for pleasure. What you need to do is organize it intelligently for your community.

Your body of work includes:

- Podcasts you record
- Videos you record
- Blog posts you create
- Newsletters you write
- Books you author
- Intellectual property you create
- Workshops you deliver
- Speeches you make
- Panels you moderate or serve on
- Client projects you complete

- Models (e.g., for problem solving) you create
- Social media postings uniquely yours
- Livestream and Zoom recorded presentations

You get the idea: You have an immense assortment of creative work to rely on and the longer you're in business, the deeper and wider it becomes.

SOCIAL PROOF

I was delivering a presentation to banking executives at a New York financial institution. At the conclusion the president stopped by, told me he loved the material, but that it must have a "shelf life" forcing me to create new work regularly. "Of course," I said. That exact same material is still in use with my clients today. Some aspects of your body of work have no expiry date!

Let's suppose your community comprises supply chain executives and managers. Your specific body of work might include charts showing that supply chains are becoming regional; a speech you made to the International Association of Supply Chain Management; two eBooks you wrote on supply chains for manufacturing and services; a monthly subscription newsletter; and processes you created to examine the quality and integrity of supply chains for any organization, regardless of industry.

List here the five most innovative and relevant aspects of your body of work that you would use to lure people to and retain people in your community:

1. ____________________
2. ____________________
3. ____________________
4. ____________________
5. ____________________

These are items of content which you can use in your promotion of the community, in live workshops, in remote presentations, in monthly newsletters, in weekly podcasts, and so forth.

HOW WILL YOU STIMULATE INVOLVEMENT?

Let's get back to "tell them you've built it and they will come."

Many people who begin formal communities are overly optimistic and too aggressive. It takes preparation and careful planning because you only are granted one first impression (hence, the purpose of this chapter).

Here are stimulus ideas and sources:

The Chain Reaction of Attraction®

Find those people (the early adapters/"hang-tens" we noted earlier) who themselves are "followed" formally or informally and invite them first. Ideally, you should know them or be introduced to them, and you should make it clear what's in it for them:

- Further recognition of their thought leadership
- Opportunity to meet peers
- "Laboratory" to test their ongoing ideas

In this way, you may bring aboard ten people, who, in turn, each attract 50 people, and suddenly you have 500. Announce to prospective members who these "originating" members are (their names and/or companies should be widely known), and have them provide a brief testimonial about why they're charter members of the community.

Pursuit of Present and Past Clients

Explain that you've treasured their partnership and you'd like to reward them with an early invitation to your community. (If you intend to charge for membership, these first two groups would be complimentary.) These people will also serve as your evangelists in the community and for prospects.

Zoom Free Session

Offer a free session on Zoom for 30 minutes laden with value, to introduce your community. However, make it clear who the desired members are so that people don't merely sign up to explore. Narrow the field (e.g., retail executives or general contractors) so that it's apparent who's appropriate. In your session, target the value accordingly.

Offer the First Year Free

If you plan to charge for membership, offer the first year free. This will overcome doubts about whether the investment has a sufficient ROI at the outset.

Bear in mind that the community, especially at the outset, is not a major money maker for you directly, but rather through the purchase of your services, evangelism, and referrals. In my case, anyone who had done business with me (not merely purchased books or audio/video) can join for free, but I charge $1,000 *for others to join for life—mine, not theirs!!*

Offer Free Inclusion for Clients

Examine your current and past clients and offer this value as your gratitude for their past and present business. (You might also offer it to prospects who did not become clients but with whom you still have positive relationships.)

Offer to Trade Associations

This can be a win/win/win whereby the association sees the potential in additional value to members, the member sees a free additional value to explore, and you receive an additional "critical mass" of members.

List here your highest potential options to stimulate involvement for your ideal members:

1. ______________________________
2. ______________________________
3. ______________________________
4. ______________________________
5. ______________________________

BENEVOLENT DICTATOR (HOW WILL YOU POSITION YOURSELF?)

You're going to be the heart and soul of the community, so be prepared for it! You may use a metaphor ("This is a teaching hospital and I'm chief of staff") or a simple set of rules, for example:

I will enforce in person and on remote platforms:

- No personal attacks on people
- Validation of statistics and claims
- Removal of sexual, religious, and/or political commentary that I deem biased or offensive

Journalist Lincoln Steffens said once, "If we had had good kings we'd still all be monarchists." I believe that a benevolent dictator is the right demeanor for maintaining a community. That means you don't take votes and don't strive for consensus. You *do* strive for innovation, diversity, and even controversy. *In the quarter century or so that I've maintained and grown my community, I've had to throw six people out. They were liars (sales advice from someone I know who never sold a thing), unethical (revealing supposedly anonymous and confidential contributions), and had mental health issues (self-loathing and attacking others).*

If you don't take action when it's required, then you'll lose respect and the offenders will drive away others. On a gentler basis, I have a series of flags I use on one of my internet platforms like the lifeguards use on beaches, the red one means that the particular thread should stop because it's been exhausted.

You'll also have to provide warnings to "play nice" when the language becomes too loud or offensive, and to question whether someone is providing "facts" or their opinions. I insist that there is no faculty at my events or in remote interactions, and that people should generally ask more questions than they try to answer. (And I caution people not to try to answer questions clearly outside of their expertise and experience.)

You may be tempted at the outset to try to appease everyone to keep them on board, but that has the opposite effect. Instead, demonstrate how the community operates and provides value, and some people might leave but the ones who stay are the ones you want.

Write down five rules you most likely want people to understand about community membership:

1. ______________________________
2. ______________________________
3. ______________________________
4. ______________________________
5. ______________________________

CONTINUAL GENERATION OF NEW VALUE AND IP (HOW WILL YOU PROVIDE IT?)

The phrase "priming the pump" originated when you poured water into the pump to stimulate well water in subsequent pumping. The same applies to the value that will attract *and sustain* people in your community. This is both a "live" and remote undertaking.

SOCIAL PROOF

Despite hundreds of recordings, people turned up to see everyone from Sinatra to Rihanna because of the experience of seeing them in person. I read Drucker's books, but I nevertheless went to hear him speak when I could.

At the outset of the community, you have to insert value continually from yourself and selected others. But this won't be spontaneous at the outset; *you have to seek it out.*

You, personally, can prime the pump with your body of work, "chunked" up for quick digestion:

- Brief podcasts
- Schedule live events
- Schedule Zoom events
- Brief videos

- Commentary on current events
- Applications of new technology
- Reviews of new management books

You get the idea. Try to provide a varied media assortment.

Meanwhile, ask your "charter members" and others to provide their ideas and commentary. You can interview some of them briefly in print of podcasts or videos. Don't expect anyone to share proprietary secrets, but do expect that they share their ideas and experiences.

You need to set this up in advance and diligently work on your and others' submissions to encourage others to contribute themselves. This will only happen if you pursue it and are disciplined about planning it.

List five ideal immediate contributions you will make or you will ask others to make to "prime the pump":

1. ______________________________
2. ______________________________
3. ______________________________
4. ______________________________
5. ______________________________

INTELLECTUAL "PRESENCE" (HOW WILL YOU DEMONSTRATE?)

As the founder of the community you are an expert in the content. That's not an admonition; that's a requirement. How do you appropriately make that "presence" manifest and evident? Here's how.

Refer to and Include Your Body of Work

We discussed the elements and sources of your body of work that will attract people. Put it on display. Refer to your publishing, recording, speaking, and even clients. Don't simply make a point, but say, "I mentioned in my weekly podcast yesterday," or "In researching my next book I found. . . ," or "I was chatting with (known expert) and we agreed that . . . ."

Make Decisions About Disputes

Settle debates that go on for too long, separate out opinion from fact and secondary sources from original sources. Make sure your own biases don't take over when someone challenges one of your positions! Make sure your position is still valid and not just something you've never challenged yourself!

Allow Your Accolades to Be Known

Talk about awards, new clients, singular experiences, and honorifics. These serve as an example for others, as well. Therefore, allow some "boasting" from others, so long as they're also participating in asking questions and admitting to needing help.

Always Include Live Events

Nothing increases credibility and respect as much as hosting a workshop, leading a mastermind group, or delivering a speech—in person.

Finally, Create and Enforce Rules

Here are the rules posted for both prospective and current members of my community.

Please remember that we are not responsible for any messages posted. We do not vouch for or warrant the accuracy, completeness, or usefulness of any message, and are not responsible for the contents of any message.

The messages express the views of the author of the message, not necessarily the views of these forums. Any user who feels that a posted message is objectionable is encouraged to contact us immediately by email. We have the ability to remove objectionable messages. and we will make every effort to do so, within a reasonable time frame, if we determine that removal is necessary.

You agree, through your use of this service, that you will not use these forums to post any material which is knowingly false and/or defamatory, inaccurate, abusive, vulgar, hateful, harassing, obscene, profane, sexually biased, threatening, invasive of a person's privacy, or otherwise violative of any law.

You agree that while using these forums there will be absolutely no smoking, and that all cell phones must be kept on silent mode.

You agree not to post others' copyrighted material without attribution and, where required, permission.

Intrusion on the board "Ask Alan" unless you are directly asking him a question will result in a $20 fine, payable to an animal welfare group, and exile from the Forums if the fine isn't promptly paid.

Write five key components from your body of work or your accomplishments or rewards and honors that you will use to create and reinforce your intellectual heft:

1. ____
2. ____
3. ____
4. ____
5. ____

ENFORCER OF RULES (WHAT WILL BE YOUR CRITERIA?)

It's important to enforce the rules or you're going to have a free-for-all. Let's call it "community policing," whereby you can warn people (please don't use that language again), sanction people (you're denied access for 30 days), or exile people (I announce who, and why).

The most frequent problem is the default to launch *ad hominem* attacks instead of debating the points. There are also problems of unsubstantiated claims, constant cynicism, and commenting in areas clearly not on one's expertise.

You can see people on a break, or offline, but you'll occasionally have to take them on in real time because *your passivity will be taken as a sign of agreement or lack of concern.*

This is why it's important in the online portion of your community to be present every day to monitor what's going on. You may have an administrator who oversees the online portion, but their job should be to alert you, not carry out instructions or penalties themselves. Among preventive actions that help are:

- Online boards where sex, religion, and politics are discussed and people know that they should expect controversial opinions if they participate there
- Anonymous contact, with the community or you, personally, where sensitive issues can be safely discussed
- Calling a break during a live session to work out something privately with an offender
- Emailing privately those who are breaking the rules of polity and support

SOCIAL PROOF

In 25 years I've had to remove six people from my community. Not one other member ever complained about any of them being told to leave.

You have to remember that your duty is to the total number of people in the community, not one person who insists on special treatment or being uncivil and hasn't respect for basic rules.

Write here the three most important rules you'll enforce and publicize in your community:

1. ______________________________
2. ______________________________
3. ______________________________

TIMING

With important events such as these you have to work "backward," from your goal to the present day. That is truly strategic. If you work from the present day forward, the deadline becomes illusive and a "moving target." If you set the specific launch date, and publicly acknowledge it and disseminate it, you are truly committed.

Zeno's Paradox: If you make progress halfway to your goal every day, you'll never reach it, because there are an infinite number of halfway points.

My experience and suggestion, having helped hundreds of people form communities, *is to choose a date six months in the future.* To some of you that will seem like a long time, and to some of you it will seem like tomorrow. You have a multitude of responsibilities, personal and professional, and you'll have resources to gather, ideas to generate, publicity to disseminate, and so on.

Some of you will have some of the prior steps completed or partially completed, and some of you will be starting for "square zero." Here's a battle plan to adjust to your personal situation and your attention to this will help you complete the exercise at the end of the chapter.

1. Who are your ideal community members?
2. What value do you want to bring to them in terms of strategy, tactics, innovation, and personal well-being?
3. What parts of your existing "body of work" fulfill those needs, and what is missing that must be developed or improved?
4. Who will be your "charter members" and evangelists, and how will you influence them to join?
5. How will you stimulate joining and involvement to achieve "critical mass" in your community?[1]
6. What types of live and remote (and other, e.g., subscriptions) offerings and when their launches will be scheduled?
7. How to impact and attract a global audience if appropriate?
8. What your role will be in monitoring interactions, administrating daily communications, enforcing rules, and generating ongoing value?
9. What you will use to keep your community contemporary and innovative continually during changing times?
10. How much time you will allocate weekly and on future offerings, live and remote?
11. What outside support you'll need and choices thereof: technology, visuals, social media promotions, legal, and so forth?
12. How you will capitalize on your success?

Once we've thoroughly prepared for, and successfully created, the launch, let's examine the ultimate success: sustainability and business growth.

Write here the first three things you will prepare in terms of intelligent timing:

1. ______________________________
2. ______________________________
3. ______________________________

NOTE

1 I recommend a minimum of at least 50 people for highly niched audiences, such as managing partners of small law firms; 100+ for larger cohorts, such as small business owners of $50 million+ firms; and 250 people for large groups such as project managers or consultants.

6

The Three Key Steps of Community Sustainability

The ecosystem is self-perpetuating when it continues to bring in new energy, new interests, and new abilities. One moves from "chief of surgery" to the CEO and hospital administrator by comparison.

EVANGELICAL IN NATURE

Your community will not grow past a given point relying solely on you or even on you and your original acolytes. There will be departures for retirement, disinterest, changed plans, changed times, personal issues, arguments, and so forth. These are to be expected. Don't pay any more attention to these as dangerous signs than you would to unsubscribers to your newsletter. (If those *do* disturb you, seek help.)

At the time of this writing, many countries (including the US, UK, Western Europe, China, Russia, and so forth) are experiencing higher morbidity rates than fertility rates. Hence, populations are decreasing and aging. In the US, by 2030, it's projected that there will be more people over 65 years of age than there will be children. That's unprecedented.[1]

Yet the US population is projected to grow from its present (2024) 330 million to about 415,00 million in the next 25 years, *of which 80+ percent of the growth will be fueled by immigration.*[2]

DOI: 10.4324/9781003507321-8

This is the analogy for your community: You must fuel it through "immigration," and here are the chief ways to create that flow:

Double-Down on the Chain Reaction of Attraction®

Try to especially please and influence those we discussed earlier who have their own set of followers. Suggest they can share their experiences and learning from the community with others, and encourage them to take a "test drive."

Go Global

Even if your ideal community members aren't international, attracting such people can make your community more appealing to the ideal members. This is their opportunity to interact with peers around the world and learn first-hand whether they share similar issues (they do) and innovative approaches to deal with them (the will).

Capture Names Relentlessly

You may well have captured names of prospective community members from meetings, associations, workshops, emails, and so forth. But you probably haven't been as efficient as you can be. Treat every inquiry as a name to capture, every introduction as a name to capture. People seldom use business cards anymore, so be sure to use your phone or a small notepad to retain information. A good idea: At any charity event or fund raiser, or industry conference, you can usually find participant names, donor names, and so on.

Use Your Web Site Aggressively (Popups)

I was never a believer in popup menus, but when my technical team persuaded me to give them a try by providing free value after anyone was on my site for ten seconds, the response was overwhelming. People thanked me for the offer (I used "11 Points of Future Potential Business," for example) and I captured highly relevant names.

Create Ever-Increasing Value in Your "Vault"

We'll talk about the Accelerant Curve in a later section, but for now be aware of (and build) "vault items," which consist of value uniquely yours which is available only within your community. Your vault should continually grow.

Co-Recruit with Synergistic Others

I wouldn't call competitors "synergistic" but I can see community owners in contracting, electrical, carpentry, and plumbing "synergistic." Similarly, credit unions, banks, and mortgage loan specialists might be ideal community members. The idea here is to build your value by introducing people in your community to other communities of value, and vice versa. My community includes coaches, consultants, trainers, speakers, and professional services people such as accountants, lawyers, and even doctors.

SOCIAL PROOF

Think about how many special interest groups you belong to on social media, and whether any of those groups (or individuals therein) can recommend other groups to you.

Maximize But Cull Your Topics (Boards)

Within your groups, whether "live" offerings or online (e.g., boards on your online platforms), seek to maximize the appeal through diverse areas of interest *but also end offerings and cull boards* where interest is waning. It might make sense to add offerings and discussions on AI in general or ChatGPT specifically, while downplaying or removing topics that are far less relevant, such as "quality teams" or "team building."

Provide Membership Options (Free and Fee)

You have to consider whether to charge for community membership, as we've discussed, along with options such as complimentary membership for charter members, for the people with a "chain reaction of attraction," and for those who participate in your workshops, events, and other offerings. You can also charge people to join as a rule or make it free as a rule.

Here's my "rule" of thumb: Keep it free at the outset, then charge as you've gained critical mass, but only for people who don't meet the criteria above. Make all membership for "life" (yours not theirs!) and don't charge annually or for renewals. The administration isn't worth it.

Remember, the more value you provide, the more people will build the community themselves and through evangelism, providing revenues for you directly and indirectly. Focus your community on value, not revenue.

Promote Guest Columns

This is one of the best mechanisms to create engagement and enthusiasm. Allow *anyone relevant* to publish on your community platforms. They needn't be members. If they're respected and known, members will appreciate the opportunity. If they are members, they will relish the opportunity to be in print (or on a podcast or in a video—I consider them all to be "publishing") and you're increasing engagement and membership.

By the way, if you also maintain blogs, newsletters, podcasts, videos, and so forth, make sure they're readily available to your community. Waiving your usual fees for any of these is another community benefit.

Publicize Community Events on Social Media

As a professional speaker, I've always thought that social media posts by a speaker proclaiming how enjoyable it was to work with a certain group *are inferior in quality to those from the group itself extolling the speaker's value.*

Encourage your community members to post on social media. This can include quotes (with attribution), events (with photos), and interactions of all kinds. You'll find yourself with scores, and later hundreds, of informal "press agents" who are publicizing the value of your community.

Write down what you will do to most promote evangelism—to create and reinforce your intellectual heft:

1. ______________________________
2. ______________________________
3. ______________________________
4. ______________________________
5. ______________________________

ACCELERANT CURVE POTENTIAL

To continue to create, present, and instantiate newer and newer value in the community, you should consider using my Accelerant Curve, seen in Figure 6.1:

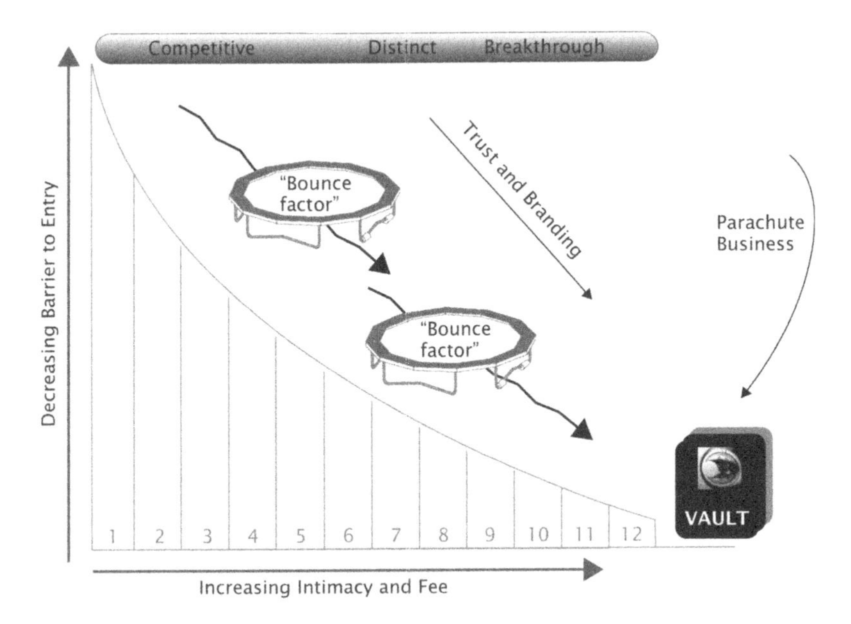

FIGURE 6.1
The Accelerant Curve.

The horizontal axis represents increasing intimacy ("high touch") and decreasing labor intensity. (It sounds like an oxymoron but it's not, read on.) The vertical axis represents barriers to, or ease of, entry into your community.

As you proceed from left to right you are progressing, for example, from free community glimpses (read certain things, but not post), to official paid or free membership, to elite membership and consistent contribution and participation. On the left you may be competitive with other communities or sources of information; in the middle, somewhat distinctive and recognizable; and on the right, unique and singular.

The "bounce factors" are interventions that move people more rapidly down the curve, such as events held with members and nonmembers (evangelism) or your body of work in the "public square" which causes people to seek you out. On the right are issues that only are available from you, hence the "vault." If your coaching is singled out and cited constantly, even though there is a plethora of coaches, your brand is a vault item. The same applies to your distinct podcasts and videos, public offerings, and even remote events.

"Parachute business" represents those who enter your community immediately on the right, so strong is your repute and so consistent are the praises and benefits concerning your community and your leadership of it.

Prospective community members will proceed more rapidly down the curve when there is trust and a highly regarded, credible brand. Let me define "brand" for you for our purposes: *A brand is how people think about you when you're not around!*

Simple as that. It means:

- People know of your community even if they don't yet belong to it.
- You and your community are cited in the media.

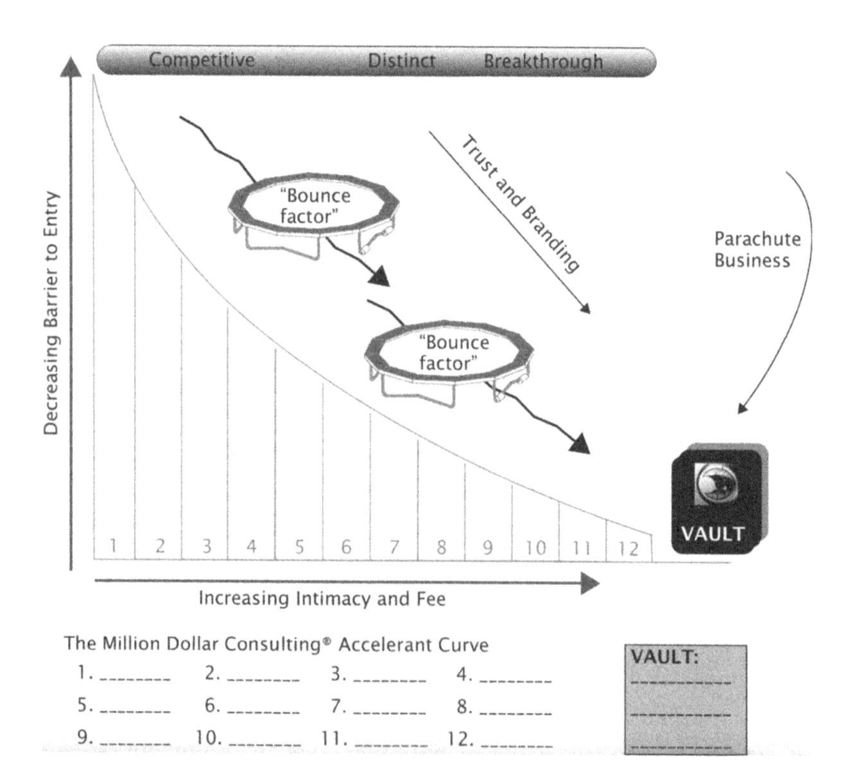

FIGURE 6.2
Accelerant curve specifics.

- People in your community are known and respected.
- In your profession and/or market, the community is creating original intellectual property and innovative ideas.
- *Members of your community are seen as being more successful than others in the profession who are not your community members.*

One of the largest detriments to community recruiting and retention is the existence of a great many highly successful people in the same profession who are blazingly successful and well known but who do not belong to the community. If you're not drawing the best and the brightest, and those very people don't feel the need to belong to your community, you have a huge public relations and image problem. That's why I've urged that you immediately recruit and romance such people in an effort to forge the chain reaction of attraction®.

We'll revisit the Acclerant Curve in Figure 6.2, but this time with the intent of your filling in 12 items along the curve, from competitive through distinctive and into breakthrough, and then three items for your "vault."

Write here your ideas for offerings on the Accelerant Curve:

OFFERINGS

1:
2:
3:
4:
5:
6:
7:
8:
9:
10:
11:
12:

VAULT ITEMS

1:
2:

DIVERSITY IN ALL FORMS

In an age where we are focused on diversity and inclusion, communities naturally serve that purpose—if you enable them to do so. Diversity of opinion is critical for any community (you want members, not acolytes), and that means a wider net, not a narrower one.

Your rules within the community should stress that no one sells to colleagues (although colleagues may request paid help from someone they think is suitable for them) or uses contact information from the community (I don't' release it) for themselves or others. However, there is nothing wrong in having "upstream" and "downstream" members.

Suppose you have an outdoor sports community. You might include:

- Amateur participants
- Professional participants
- Equipment suppliers
- Site owners
- Medical experts
- Nutritional experts
- Indoor practice and workout facility owners
- Food supplement providers
- Travel planners
- Tour guides
- Coaches
- Course designers
- Therapists
- Mental health professionals
- Clothing and accessory providers
- EMTs

I enjoy healthy arguments and debates within my community, and I'm sure the participants do as well, or they wouldn't be so active in them! As I write this, Pickle Ball is the current craze. A lot of middle-aged (and older) people are enjoying the game, grabbing new equipment, adorning themselves with new fashions—and getting injured in a manner they never considered. (And something called "Padel Ball" is coming.)

Thus, the diversity on my list above makes for a comprehensive gathering of all aspects of outdoor sports, from emergencies on a ski slope to hitting a gap wedge, and from properly warming up to properly cooling down.

In a business sense, if your community were focused on the consumer retail business, you might include:

- Manufacturers
- Designers
- Store owners
- Store employees
- Customers
- "Influencers"
- Makeup and grooming experts
- Media, PR, and advertising experts

From the very diversity and inclusion, you can create communities where people related to the topic and values *can't afford NOT to be members.*

There are about 19,000 model train clubs and communities in the US and Canada[3] and about 500,000 people engaged in the hobby which generates about $450 million annually! And that's just one hobby where the average age of members is probably well past 60![4]

You have to use a wide net and not be overly niched in your choice of community members. Let's say you chose managing partners of boutique legal firms (fewer than a dozen attorneys). There are about 450,000 law firms in the US and that number grows by almost one percent annually.[5,6] Most of them are small firms. And then there are attorneys at larger firms who would like to go out on their own, expert witnesses (yes, it's a profession) who would be interested, legal supply houses, technology companies, and on and on.

I've found that attorneys are like amoeba, constantly splitting and forming new entities (and taking clients with them, the same way manicurists or hairstylists do when they open their own shops).

By accepting veterans and neophytes, producers and customers, and the great variety of related parties we've been discussing, you are also far more assured of diversity in terms of:

- Global locations
- Ethnic and racial diversity

- Large and small operations
- Mentors and mentees
- Conservative and liberal approaches
- The gamut of experiences in the area
- Lifestyle varieties
- Diversity in evangelism
- Maximizing the chain reaction of attraction®

Write down the five most important sources of diversity that you will focus on in forming and sustaining your community:

1. ______________________________
2. ______________________________
3. ______________________________
4. ______________________________
5. ______________________________

NOTES

1 https://www.census.gov/newsroom/press-releases/2018/cb18-41-population-projections.html#:~:text=6%2C%202018%20—%20The%20year%202030,residents%20will%20be%20retirement%20age.
2 https://www.brookings.edu/articles/new-census-projections-show-immigration-is-essential-to-the-growth-and-vitality-of-a-more-diverse-us-population/
3 https://www.railserve.com/Models/Clubs/North_America/US_Canada/
4 https://www.google.com/search?client=safari&sca_esv=cea3cab0966c3853&rls=en&q=How+many+model+train+enthusiasts+are+there%3F&sa=X&ved=2ahUKEwiDkbmiyoCFAxVig4kEHV5fDwoQzmd6BAgSEAY&biw=1627&bih=965&dpr=2
5 https://www.statista.com/statistics/822025/us-legal-services-market-law-firms/
6 Knopf, 2006.

Part Three

Specialized Applications for the Future

7

Specialized Communities

I've built these cross-functionally and among different markets, but also within markets. This is a specialty chapter for those wanting to build community in vertical markets and specialty areas.

NONPROFITS

Nonprofits need to build communities for these critical reasons:

- Donors are critical for unearned income.
- Board members of substantial expertise are needed.
- Volunteers to provide free labor are essential.
- Media coverage and PR are required.

SOCIAL PROOF

Too many nonprofits "burn up" volunteers on minor matters and small fundraisers, like cake sales, instead of focusing them on major efforts, such as formal auctions, sponsorships, scholarships, and so forth. Volunteers are great assets, and they must be applied against great potential.

Here is an instance of a community progressing beyond its original intent. The March of Dimes was begun in 1938 in response to President Franklin D. Roosevelt's polio diagnosis. It was originally called the National Foundation for Infantile Paralysis. Every year, when I was in grammar school in the early 1950s, we were asked to contribute a dime or more toward this cause.

DOI: 10.4324/9781003507321-10

However, unlike cancer, where we are focused overwhelmingly on contingent actions and treating the disease, polio was effectively prevented with the introduction of vaccines beginning in 1955. So, did the March of Dime go out of business?

It did not. It had an effective infrastructure, a network of fundraising and volunteers, and a highly positive public image. After all, it had helped eliminate polio through its fundraising. *So it reoriented its community to the health of babies and the prevention of birth defects and infant mortality.*

In 2023, the March of Dimes had revenues of about $170 million and is going strong in its new mission and the continuation of its community. This is largely a volunteer-run organization.

We've seen arts groups grow from local to regional to national, private schools go from primary to secondary education, and community advocacy groups go from local issues to national issues.

Many parents, concerned about the efficacy and safety and emotional support of public school education, have opted for private schools. These aren't merely wealthy people; these are people who seek scholarships and nonsecular schools. The schools have responded in kind.

For example, many non-Catholics send their children to Catholic schools, highly regarded for the thoroughness of the academics and the discipline for behavior and accountability. The tuition is relatively inexpensive compared to secular private schools. The requirement to take a class or classes in religion is accepted by these parents as part of the learning and also part of the "price" of admission. The schools do not demand conversion or religious commitments outside of school.

We can see in both the March of Dimes and private schools the power of community beyond the actual *raison d'être* of the community.

There are arts groups that were engaged in ballet that have expanded into contemporary dance and formed collaborations with symphonies and regional theaters. Boy Scout and Girl Scout merit badges have progressed from "reading" and "cooking" to "citizenship" and "environmental science."

I noted earlier that pychologist Dan Gilbert of Harvard, in his book *Stumbling on Happiness*,[6] discussed research which proved that people who stated they believed in God were no happier than people who stated they did not believe in God. However, people who stated that they attended church were significantly happier than those who stated they did not.

Gilbert's conclusion is that it was a sense of community that generated the happiness of the church attendees, not the belief in the deity. That belief is what brought them to church, but it was the church as community that created their happiness.

If you are working in a nonprofit, or on the board, or contribute to one, what five areas should it most focus on in building a synergistic community:

1. ______________________________
2. ______________________________
3. ______________________________
4. ______________________________
5. ______________________________

EDUCATION

A very good friend of mine, Dr. Nido Qubein, has been president of High Point University in High Point, North Carolina, since 2005. The school announced a ten-year growth plan of $2 billion in 2019, and, in 2022 alone, it was announced that three families had donated $100 million in just 30 days. His tenure has produced at least $800 million in fundraising without a capital campaign.

A Comment on Success

> The expansion continues the United Methodist-affiliated university's dramatic growth since longtime High Point businessman Qubein became president in 2005. What was a 92-acre campus is now 550 acres, with more than 100 buildings constructed and about a dozen new schools added to three existing ones when Qubein arrived. Enrollment has grown from 1,400 *to* 6,300, including about 1,500 graduate students. Annual revenue totals $500 million, producing cash flow of about $100 million, the president said.

You might say that Nido is a superb businessman, and you'd be right. You might say that he's a gifted fund-raiser and highly generous himself, and you'd be right. But you'd also be right if you observed that he knows how to build a community.

The average four-year college graduation rate in the US is 60 percent. At High Point it's 75 percent. They build new schools and facilities with huge fundraising, not exorbitant tuition. And do it all without debt. The students all know the president and happily greet him when he travels around the campus. He personally teaches a class for 1500 freshmen.

People donate to this community not just because it provides huge economic growth for the surrounding communities but because they want to be a part of the legacy of learning and individual growth that the school provides.

SOCIAL PROOF

This university community is not bounded by its campus or its students, or its facilities. It has created an existential community.

Peter Drucker remarked once (and I'm paraphrasing) that an organization is not like a cheetah or a tulip, successful merely by perpetuating the species. It is successful only by the contribution it makes to the environment. He wasn't talking about the current "environmentalism" but rather the communities in which people live and work, the culture and the interactions.

This holds true even more so for education. We all pay taxes for public schools whether or not we have children in them at the time, and whether or not we even have children, and whether or not we have children whom we send to private schools (as we discussed above with a choice for secular schooling). Why is this "fair"?

Because we *all* benefit from educating our children to become effective, contributing (and tax-paying) members of society. In fact, it's highly apparent today that every child who does not have equal opportunity to acquire a high-quality education at primary and secondary levels has a high chance of becoming *a future social liability and expense* because of poor employment or unemployment, crime, drugs, homelessness, addiction, ill health, and even suicide.

Remember Hillary Clinton's comment that "It takes a village" (which originates in an African proverb, "It takes a village to raise a child")? Education, even at university and post-graduate levels, can't be left to secluded, tenured, monk-like, aloof "experts." It has to be community-supported because it's for the benefit of the community. But I'm not talking about a physical, geographic community but rather the community of that school and the ramifications of its education.

Penn State (best known perhaps, for football) has about 700,000 alumni. Think of their (and their descendants') potential impact on society and the world.

It's incumbent upon the school to recognize its community-building potential and to instantiate and sustain it. *That is inclusion.* It's a combination of alumni, students, faculty, parents, employees, and donors. It's a community that will enable a faster, better achievement of its vision and goals.

If you don't believe that, just ask Nido Qubein.

If you work in education, or are an alumni, or are in school, or are a parent, or are a taxpayer (just about everyone is relevant), what do you think are the five things an institution should focus on to develop the community it already has in place, whether it's apparent of not:

1. ____________________
2. ____________________
3. ____________________
4. ____________________
5. ____________________

HEALTHCARE

Healthcare is "famous" for communities, and somewhat "infamous" for not making the best of them.

There are communities around common illnesses and diseases, patient-facing professionals, specialized doctors, fads (cosmetic surgery, Ozempic for weight loss, Botox, and so forth), and hospitals and their support (children's, veterans', Ronald MacDonald House).

My twin grandchildren were born two weeks on the side of viable and spent a long time in the NICU (neonatal intensive care unit). My daughter is still friendly with other parents who were with their children in the unit—16 years ago.

The community is widening, because telehealth is bringing patients together with medical people at great distances. You might have a dermatologist in Manila examining a mole on your finger at your home in South Dakota. Expert heart surgeons in Boston, via closed circuit TV and the internet, attend and collaborate with surgeons in the operating rooms throughout New England.

When I say "infamous" I mean that nurses, in particular, have rightly complained about being treated as second-class citizens and not listened to by doctors. Yet today, patients are seeing more and more highly skilled nurse practitioners and thereby freeing up doctors' time. And I've met too many people—and had too many experiences—with a medical operations' front office staffs who are rude, insensitive, and indifferent. In one office, with waiting patients nervously sitting and worrying about diagnoses for themselves and/or their loved ones, the staff was eating snacks at their desks and laughing loudly. At another, patient files were left in plain view on the clerk's desk, a violation of US HIPA laws (Health Insurance Portability and Accountability Act of 1996).

As an example of these communities expanding, more and more responsibility has been placed on pharmacists—namely, providing vaccinations, suggesting lower priced genetic drugs, recommending over-the-counter preparations, recommending courses of action and behavior. (Just to expand this somewhat bizarrely, large pet stores such as PetSmart, in addition to pet food, toys, leashes, beds, and so forth, also have onsite groomers and veterinarians available. How long before the CVS in your town has a doctor in residence?)

Think of the efficiencies gained and errors averted if now-informal communities were more formalized. Candidates for membership by profession, or geography, or specialization might include:

- Doctors
- Nurses
- Front office staff
- Intake and discharge staff
- Pharmacists
- Pharmaceutical company representatives
- Patient advocacy groups
- Advocates for homeless and indigent
- Medical school faculty
- Hospital employees (transporters, orderlies, etc.)
- EMTs
- Physical therapists
- Psychotherapists

- Medical equipment suppliers
- Patients and patient advocacy groups
- Insurers

This might sound *too* inclusive and perhaps it is, but if even half of these potential community members could find a common place to talk, interact, exchange ideas, compare techniques, seek cost saving, and create better practices—well, what's that worth?

Healthcare is an excellent example of both vertical and horizontal potential for prospective community members.

Have you ever seen a doctor's personal desk, real or electronic? It's often "piled" with magazines, extracts, and newsletters that the doctor knows ought to be read but never quite finds the time to read them. The need for comparison of best practices in this profession is huge, and anyone founding and hosting a community within the profession can provide a huge service.

Never forget, the value implicit in communities is in bringing people together who otherwise wouldn't know each other. And I'll suggest that just because people work in one building and in one profession doesn't mean they know *each other.*

SOCIAL PROOF

When my wife had a hip replacement and I visited her in the hospital, there was a huge white board on the wall of her room. On it was a notice provided by the staff: "Don't forget to ask your doctors if they've washed their hands before examining you!" That's an example of a non-hierarchical, mutually supportive community.

What are the first five groups or professions you'd try to recruit for your healthcare community?

1. ____________________
2. ____________________
3. ____________________
4. ____________________
5. ____________________

8

The Future of Community Building

The best and most fruitful communities are those that change with the times and even anticipate the approaching times. They create disruption and turmoil. Their members are thought leaders and icons.

LEVERAGING THE TUMULT OF THE TIMES

The Covid disruption is moving farther and farther away. There are still people contracting it, and "long Covid" has devastating effects. However, it's no longer an "excuse" for keeping a low profile.

In fact, what we learned from it is a reason to become high profile.

SOCIAL PROOF

When Covid hit I called the three financial advisors who handle different aspects of my investments. I asked each, independently, what course of action to follow. They all asked me the same question: "Do you have cash?" I told them I did. "Then do nothing different," each one said. "Just call us if you need cash." All three knew that something *was going to create turmoil at some point and they were prepared for it. They just didn't know that it would be a microbe.*

There is no "return to normal" after a global crisis, nor the deceptive call for a "new normal." Instead, we are operating in an environment of No Normal®, which I've trademarked because it's such an important concept.

DOI: 10.4324/9781003507321-11

Communities can't be based on some return to a remembered and attractive past, nor trying to recreate it. Billy Joel famously sang, "The good ole days weren't always good, and tomorrow ain't as bad as it seems" (Keeping the Faith, 1983). We are living in continually turbulent and disruptive times when volatility is omnipresent.

You can look at geopolitics, athletic upsets, the stock market, elections, AI, climate change, and a host of other realities around us to understand that change is accelerating and we can't just react to it—*we have to anticipate it and exploit it.*

I mean "exploit" in the most positive manner: capitalize on it, improve our lives because of it, and help people improve from it. That's the societal and business equivalent of "Do you have cash?"

Let's look at some of the great organizational success stories. These are organizations which utilized volatility and disruption to better serve their constituencies.

Dyson is not a vacuum cleaner company. It is in the *air movement* business. They do make very effective vacuums, but they also make state-of-the-art hair dryers, hand dryers, and so forth. If they believed they simply make vacuum cleaners, they wouldn't be so successful or well known.

SOCIAL PROOF

IBM, which stands for International Business Machine, is not in the business machine or computer business. It is in the information exchange business, and most of its profit comes from consulting, not manufacturing or software.

When the late Herb Kelleher founded and first ran Southwest Airlines, there were no baggage fees and no frills, the flight attendants often hid in the overhead bins, and everyone had a lot of fun. Kelleher was a chain-smoking, hard-drinking guy, but he forged a highly successful, low-cost airline which served tens of millions of people well. With his departure, the airline doesn't stand out in a crowd anymore and has fallen on harder times. (As I write this, the airline has announced it's abandoning its famed "open seating" arrangement and is selling seats with extra leg room.)

Ameritrade and Schwab built organizations which allowed investors to make very inexpensive stock trades in their homes, on their phones, and avoid the previously daunting higher commission rates. They didn't invent stock trading; they simply made it practical for the masses.

And what if you don't do this? Recently, the government sued the real estate industry through the once-powerful National Association of Realtors and won a $418 million judgment—and the reality of much lower costs for home buyers and sellers—because the association and the profession had operated for decades based on an arbitrary six percent commission system. The profession simply sailed along, not trying to disrupt the market, so the market was disrupted for them.

Many experts calculate a savings *in the billions of dollars* over the ensuing year for home transactions. The moral here is that if you don't create volatility and disruption to the benefit of your customers and yourself, you're likely to wind up on the wrong end of it due to competitive actions.

SOCIAL PROOF

In the mid-1990s I pioneered value-based pricing for consultants, replacing the old "time and materials" standards based on the longer a consultant stayed—which is detrimental to the client—the more the consultant made. Thirty years later I still have the most powerful solo consulting brand in the world.

What are the disruptive and volatile *positive* actions and ideas you can introduce to help your ideal clients and community members to better attract people:

1. ______________________________
2. ______________________________
3. ______________________________
4. ______________________________
5. ______________________________

AGILITY AND RESILIENCE TO BOUNCE FORWARD

Resilience is the ability to recover quickly from difficulties. Agility is the ability to move quickly and easily. Hence, this section is about the ability to quickly and easily recover from setbacks *and bounce forward*. After all, if you're not losing at times, you're not learning. That learning should drive you forward from the setback, not bounce you backward.

Let's isolate this in Figure 8.1:

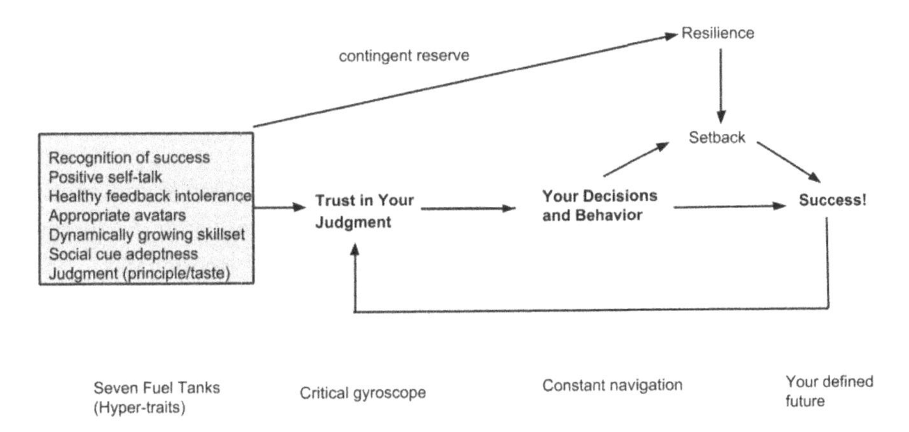

FIGURE 8.1
Community resilience.

You must have trust in your own judgment for that people in your community will trust your judgment (and learn to trust their own).

That trust leads to better behaviors and successful decision making, resulting in success. It's on this journey that setbacks can occur (you give bad advice, there's a failed community event, someone complains about poor treatment, and so forth) which should be treated as learning points *for everyone* so that you easily bounce forward on the success track.

The chart depicts what I call "hyper-traits" which provide the fuel for this progression and the necessary reserve or safety valve when you do fact setback. I've called this the "contingent reserve," which you can call upon when you need to overcome obstacles or "right a wrong."

Hyper-Traits

Recognition of success: Creating and understanding the metrics for success and focusing on excellence not perfection. Understanding that there are ranges of success.

Positive self-talk: The ability to create instant perspective. If a proposal is rejected you don't say, "I'm a lousy marketer," but rather. "At his time, in this place, with this person, I didn't succeed. Let me try to find out why so that I don't repeat the experience."

Healthy feedback intolerance: You read that correctly. You can't listen to unsolicited feedback, which is always for the sender. You should confine yourself to feedback from people you trust and ask and be comfortable only with that.

Appropriate avatars: Whom do you look to as an exemplar of the behavior and success you seek, and are you serving in that capacity for community members?

Dynamically growing skillset: Are you gaining in competence and confidence? Can you do things today better than yesterday or do things today you couldn't do at all yesterday, mentally and emotionally?

Social cue adeptness: Can you recognize what is happening around you, and are you "in the moment" rather than following a mental script or "acting" instead of being authentic? Do you know and are you sensitive enough to understand that you need to change your behavior and approaches immediately?

Judgment (principle and taste): Thomas Jefferson said, "In matters of taste go with the tide, in matters of principle stand like a rock." Can you discriminate between the two? To put it bluntly, do you know when to compromise and when to stand your ground?

These traits can be developed and refined continually so that your resilience is always powerful and available.

SOCIAL PROOF

I was running a very high-end, high-fee session for elite clients on thought leadership. My guest speaker had written a well-received book on leadership, but I had never met her.

She turned out to be, during her presentation, a cynical, depressing person with a negative worldview. She was an activist early in her career and felt important goals had never been met and never would be. When she left, after light, polite applause, everyone stared at me wondering what on earth I could say to justify my choice of a guest at these high prices.

I said: "Well, we have an important lesson here: I couldn't have arranged it any better. She and I are contemporaries, are the same age, had some of the same clients, and went through the same times. I'm an extremely optimistic guy trying to show people the opportunities and worth all over this wonderful country. She's someone who's so desperately unhappy that she won't be happy until you're unhappy.

"Whom would you rather expose your children to in school, hire as a coach, employ as a consultant, or even trust and rely upon as a colleague?"

The group applauded loudly and we then had an hour's discussion on how people can make the best or worst of conditions around them, which was completely within their power either way.

That's how resilience can help you to bounce forward.

List here three of the "hyper-traits" that you feel you have to develop with the best return of improving yourself and your community's resilience;

1. ______________________________
2. ______________________________
3. ______________________________

MAXIMIZING VALUE TO MAXIMIZE PROFITS

Although your community can make an enormous amount of money for you, and you can provide diverse offerings as seen on the aforementioned Accelerant Curve, the key to your future is *continually adding value.* If members feel they're simply experiencing the "same old/same old," they will visit less, evangelize less, and eventually drop out.

Online, on your platforms and blog and newsletters, you should apprise members of new value—from you or their colleagues. You can arrange for online platforms to notify members of new posts. I don't like that "clutter" when people already receive far too many emails, so my primary online platform, AlansForums.com, has a button to click for "unread posts." That way, someone who visits once a day or who hasn't been able to visit for a week can readily determine "what's new."

You can pump new value into the community frequently (and I'm talking a minimum of weekly and would prefer daily) by doing the following.

Creating Case Studies

These should be actual experiences you've had in your work where you don't have to cite the names (unless you have permission). An excellent case study should have three brief elements:

1. Situation
   Example: A $4 million boutique professional services company owner found that he was exhausted as the sole rainmaker and was supporting a dozen delivery people.
2. Intervention
   Example: We interviewed present and past clients and prospects who did not sign on. We found that, universally, the owner and his repute were the "draw" and the implementation wasn't differentiated from other firms. Those who did not sign on were concerned that the owner would not work with them one-on-one and didn't want to go through his subordinates.
3. Resolution
   Example: We changed the business model to an advisory (as opposed to project-based) approach, eliminated all but one employee for purposes of research and prospecting, and provided messaging and scripts to promote our client as the sole person to work with a client executive and expect it to be largely remote, not on site. This not only reduced our client's labor intensity but increased his personal income by over $300,000.

You can see how these case studies are easily created and shared, and can be applied to members' businesses and professions across the board.

Provide Incentive for Members to Contribute Value

People are often afraid to reveal their techniques and models because they fear "theft" and competitive measures. Yet you can disprove that by demonstrating that people who have written books have displayed all of their IP in public *because people seek the sources and then recognize that you are the source.* No one wants a copycat. (And no one ever learned to skip by reading a book.)

Moreover, community members are prone to trust sharing because they've been interacting within the community both in person and remotely. Finally, the credit they receive from good ideas is rewarding for egos and status.

Provide Contests and Exercises

Offer challenges, games, and exercises with a time limit for response (to accommodate all time zones, however) so that people have to develop their own resolutions. Emphasize that there are no "right or wrong" answers but that people have to justify their recommendations and how they would be implemented.

An alternative to doing this is to take contemporary news stories and challenge the group to resolve them. (We talked about the Suez Canal being blocked, supply chains disrupted, and what the most effective preventive and contingent actions might be. Many people suggested regionalizing supply chains, and that's exactly what's happened in actuality.)

Use Live Events as a Practicum

I like to ask hotel management to give us their major problems so that we can assign members of the group to work on them during our time in workshops. Management loves the "free help" and we get to deal with "live" issues. As an example of just one such exercise, we helped a Ritz Carlton ready suites for VIP guests much faster by changing housekeeping protocols and ended a bottleneck at the circular entrance by changing the practice of the same employees both receiving new guests and retrieving cars for current guests. (It was counterintuitive but it worked!)

These are ways to maintain a "waterfall" of value and new ideas flowing that encourage members to stay and contribute and are excellent attractions for new members.

In what ways will you best stimulate ongoing, challenging value and ideas in your community?

1. ______________________________
2. ______________________________
3. ______________________________
4. ______________________________
5. ______________________________

BUILD IT, *TELL THEM YOU'VE BUILT IT,* AND THEY WILL COME

I've mentioned this before, but I want to conclude the book with this premise: *Shameless Promotion*. The quote above comes from *Field of Dreams*, which is the story of a farmer who builds a baseball park in a cornfield which then attracts the ghosts of legends of the game.

The premise is based on the ghosts knowing the field, and it's been misappropriated to suggest that if you build anything well enough, it will attract the right people. *But since we're dealing with people and not ghosts, we can't rely on their telepathic abilities.* We need to tell them what we've built.

Hence, we need to assertively promote our community. We would have done this to a certain extent during the launch, of course, and with our sustaining tactics as discussed earlier.

However, conditions change and there are always people who become "eligible" for our communities who may well not know they exist. (And just as the morbidity rate of many advanced countries is exceeding fertility rates so that immigration is required to fill all kinds of jobs, you can't allow retirements, illnesses, job changes, and so forth to deplete your community without a constant "immigration" of new people.)

If your community reaches an equilibrium, a plateau wherein new people are exactly replacing departing people, you have a problem because all plateaus erode due to the laws of entropy. The way to avoid this is to seek constant growth, and the secret to constant growth is constant innovation. Figure 8.2 shows how this is accomplished.

Your community will probably have slow growth at startup as you try to recruit key people and rely on the chain reaction of attraction®. However, dynamic growth should follow as evangelism takes hold and your efforts become publicized.

Then, as in all fast-growing endeavors, a critical juncture occurs. As growth slows you may regard your current status as wonderful as compared to your community origins and simply begin to "coast" for a while. But what appears to you to be a success plateau is actually the beginning of a success trap.

All plateaus will eventually erode because of the law of entropy (a gradual decline into disorder). The way to avoid this is through constant growth, which we've explained requires constant innovation. This means that while you are growing, *but you notice the rate of growth slowing, you must "jump"*

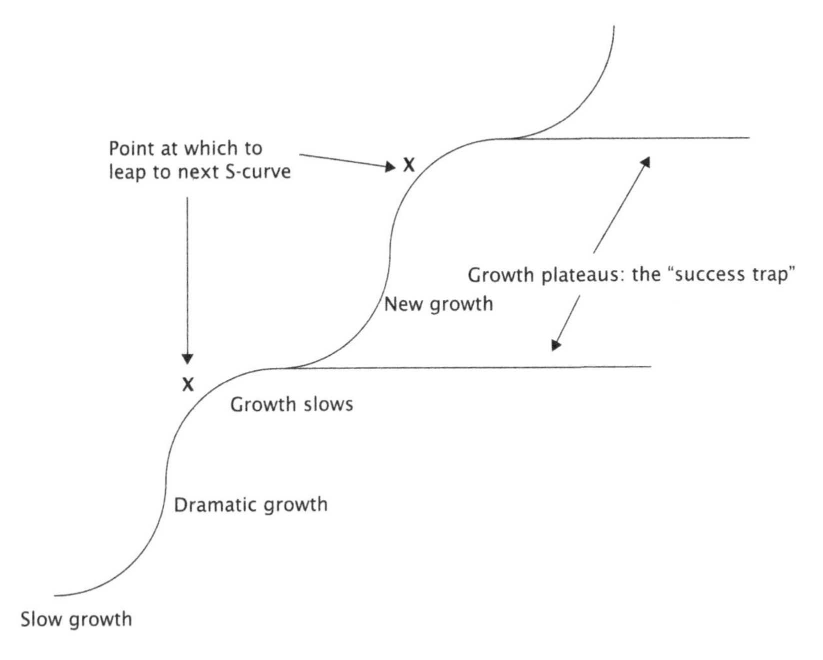

FIGURE 8.2
The S-curve and "success trap."

to the next S-curve. That "jump" will require innovation: new offerings, new experiences, dramatic new IP, new recruitment efforts.

When you are successful, after another rather slow introduction of these efforts, you'll experience more dramatic growth. As you can see in the chart, *it's relatively easy to make that small jump when you have the tremendous momentum of growth fueling you. But if you ignore the ideal jump spot, the further you go on the plateau, the greater the jump to the next S-curve and with far less momentum.* At some point it becomes impossible and your community will wither and fail.

Hence, the "success trap."

So remember to build it and keep telling people you've built it, and then keep reminding them at your "jump spot" that you've built still more, better, and important value.

SOCIAL PROOF

The only way you're able to "coast" is by doing downhill, and community building is an uphill pursuit at all times. Keep pedaling; keep climbing.

What measures will you introduce and implement to ensure you jump to the next S-curve when you see indications that growth is starting to decline?

1. ____________________
2. ____________________
3. ____________________
4. ____________________
5. ____________________

Epilogue: The Game Plan

I've assembled your "assignments" in order here to create a roadmap for success, from your ideas about community to the creation, sustaining, and continuing dramatic growth of your community. You can find these electronically on my site if that's more convenient for you: (alanweiss.com)

What are three key attributes or strengths that you have as a community organizer?

1. ____
2. ____
3. ____

My ideal community member:

____

____

Write below why you seek to form a community (or improve a current one):

____

____

Write below the values you'll provide:

____

____

What are the primary values for you to acquire/achieve in your community?

1. ____
2. ____
3. ____

DOI: 10.4324/9781003507321-12

Write down five issues that you think are, or will be, of significant importance and interest to your community members:

1. ______________________________
2. ______________________________
3. ______________________________
4. ______________________________
5. ______________________________

Write down five improved conditions that you think are, or will be, of significant importance and interest to your specific community members:

1. ______________________________
2. ______________________________
3. ______________________________
4. ______________________________
5. ______________________________

Write down five education/entertainment/experiential options that you think are, or will be, of significant importance and interest to your specific community members:

1. ______________________________
2. ______________________________
3. ______________________________
4. ______________________________
5. ______________________________

Write down five techniques you'd use to maximize members' opportunities to meet each other and interact:

1. ______________________________
2. ______________________________
3. ______________________________
4. ______________________________
5. ______________________________

Write down five access points and interactive devices you'd use to address such problem areas:

1. ______________________________
2. ______________________________

3. ______________________________
4. ______________________________
5. ______________________________

Write down five experiences that you've had, positive and negative, that you would share as empirical evidence in your community:

1. ______________________________
2. ______________________________
3. ______________________________
4. ______________________________
5. ______________________________

Write down five experiences you'll consider, live or remote, to entice people to voluntarily keep returning to your community events and offerings:

1. ______________________________
2. ______________________________
3. ______________________________
4. ______________________________
5. ______________________________

Whom do you wish to attract to your community by job title?

List here your five most innovative and relevant aspects of your body of work that you would use to lure people to and retain people in your community:

1. ______________________________
2. ______________________________
3. ______________________________
4. ______________________________
5. ______________________________

List here your highest potential options to stimulate involvement for your ideal members:

1. ______________________________
2. ______________________________
3. ______________________________
4. ______________________________
5. ______________________________

Write down five rules you most likely want people to understand about community membership:

1. ______
2. ______
3. ______
4. ______
5. ______

List five ideal immediate contributions you will make or you will ask others to make to "prime the pump":

1. ______
2. ______
3. ______
4. ______
5. ______

Write five key components from your body of work or your accomplishments or rewards and honors that you will use to create and reinforce your intellectual heft:

1. ______
2. ______
3. ______
4. ______
5. ______

Write here the three most important rules you'll enforce and publicize in your community:

1. ______
2. ______
3. ______

Write here the first three things you will prepare in terms of intelligent timing:

1. ______
2. ______
3. ______

Write down what you will do to most promote evangelism:

1. ____
2. ____
3. ____
4. ____
5. ____

Write here your ideas for offerings on the Accelerant Curve:

OFFERINGS

1:
2:
3:
4:
5:
6:
7:
8:
9:
10:
11:
12:

VAULT ITEMS

1:
2:

Write down the five most important sources of diversity that you will focus on in forming and sustaining your community:

1. ____
2. ____
3. ____
4. ____
5. ____

If you are working in a nonprofit, or on the board, or contribute to one, what five areas should it most focus on in building a synergistic community:

1. ______
2. ______
3. ______
4. ______
5. ______

If you work in education, or are an alumnus, or are in school, or are a parent, or are a taxpayer (just about everyone is relevant), what are the five things that you consider the institution should focus on to develop the community it already has in place, whether it's apparent or not:

1. ______
2. ______
3. ______
4. ______
5. ______

What are the first five groups or professions you'd try to recruit for your healthcare community?

1. ______
2. ______
3. ______
4. ______
5. ______

What are the disruptive and volatile *positive* actions and ideas you can introduce to help your ideal clients and community members to better attract people:

1. ______
2. ______
3. ______
4. ______
5. ______

List here three of the "hyper-traits" that you feel you have to develop with the best return of improving yourself and your community's resilience:

1. ______________________________
2. ______________________________
3. ______________________________

In what ways will you best stimulate ongoing, challenging value and ideas in your community?

1. ______________________________
2. ______________________________
3. ______________________________
4. ______________________________
5. ______________________________

What measures will you introduce and implement to ensure you jump to the next S-curve when you see indications that growth is starting to decline?

1. ______________________________
2. ______________________________
3. ______________________________
4. ______________________________
5. ______________________________

WHEN WILL I BEGIN: ______________

Index

Page numbers in *italics* indicate a figure on the corresponding page.

Printed in the United States
by Baker & Taylor Publisher Services